B. Teufel / S. Schmidt / T. Teufel

C^2
Compiler Concepts

Springer-Verlag   Wien NewYork

Dr. Bernd Teufel
ART Informationssysteme GmbH, Überlingen

Dr. Stephanie Schmidt
Institut für Informatik, Universität Zürich,

Prof. Dr. Thomas Teufel
Arbeitsbereich Technische Informatik III, Technische Universität Hamburg-Harburg

Printed on acid-free paper

With 70 Figures

ISBN-13: 978-3-211-82431-3   e-ISBN-13: 978-3-7091-9274-0
DOI: 10.1007/978-3-7091-9274-0

Preface

Writing a compiler is a very good practice for learning how complex problems could be solved using methods from software engineering. It is extremely important to program rather carefully and exactly, because we have to remember that a compiler is a program which has to handle an input that is usually incorrect. Therefore, the compiler itself must be error-free.

Referring to Niklaus Wirth, we postulate that the grammatical structure of a language must be reflected in the structure of the compiler. Thus, the complexity of a language determines the complexity of the compiler (cf. *Compilerbau*. B. G. Teubner Verlag, Stuttgart, 1986).

This book is about the translation of programs written in a high level programming language into machine code. It deals with all the major aspects of compilation systems (including a lot of examples and exercises), and was outlined for a one session course on compilers. The book can be used both as a teacher's reference and as a student's text book. In contrast to some other books on that topic, this text is rather concentrated to the point. However, it treats all aspects which are necessary to understand how compilation systems will work.

Chapter One gives an introductory survey of compilers. Different types of compilation systems are explained, a general compiler environment is shown, and the principle phases of a compiler are introduced in an informal way to sensitize the reader for the topic of compilers.

Chapter Two may be thought of as the definition module of the text. Terminology for grammars and languages as well as basic analysing techniques are introduced. Finally, the definition of the programming language PL/0 is given – this language will be used in the following Chapters to explain particular methods. PL/0 was introduced by Niklaus Wirth as an example of a very simple programming language consisting of all important structures and features to exemplify and demonstrate the major compiler concepts. Since this language fulfils this purpose very good, we did neither choose another more complex language, such as PASCAL or MODULA-2, nor did we define our own language to have a medium for demonstration.

Chapter Three is about lexical analysis and organization of symbol tables. Since finite automata are very convenient models for describing how the symbols of formal languages (generated by regular grammars, cf. Chapter 2) should be analyzed, an introduction to finite automata is given before scanners themselves are considered. Symbol tables as a compiler's central information structure are introduced and several forms for their organization are discussed. Finally, the code for lexical analysis of PL/0 is given.

Chapter Four deals with parsers. The Chapter is subdivided according to the two principal analyzing techniques: Top-down analysis and bottom-up analysis. The most efficient top-down and bottom-up parsers are based on context-free LL-grammars and LR-grammars, respectively. Thus, those grammars are introduced before the parsing methods themselves are explained. Both analysing methods are introduced using simple examples. Finally, the code for a recursive descent parser for PL/0 is given.

Chapter Five considers the semantic meaning of programs: Semantic and type analysis. Syntactical structures of a source code are semantically analyzed by interpreting the meaning of that source code, i.e. by generating an internal representation of the source code. Several forms of internal representations (intermediate codes) are discussed before techniques of syntax-directed translation and type checking are introduced. Finally, a code fragment for the generation of an intermediate code for PL/0 is given.

Chapter Six is about error handling. Compilers are systems which in most cases have to deal with an incorrect input. Thus, error handling is an important part of a compiler. Possible errors are characterized and classified before error handling and recovery techniques for lexical and syntactical analysis are discussed. Finally, several techniques are exemplified considering again PL/0.

Chapter Seven is about code generation and code optimization. Storage allocation techniques (static, stack, and heap allocation), parameter passing, as well as addressing methods are explained. Code generation is that part of a compiler which strongly depends on the target hardware. However, some basic steps are common to every code generation phase and, therefore, a general code generation algorithm is introduced. Finally, major optimization techniques are discussed.

Chapter Eight concludes this book with a few remarks on the influences of hardware development on programming language and compiler design.

A great number of *Exercises* is separately included to allow the reader to assess his understanding of the book's content.

Acknowledgement

We would like to thank Anke John for her numerous valuable comments. Her interest and encouragement in this book are appreciated greatly.

Bernd Teufel   Ulm

Stephanie Schmidt   Zürich

Thomas Teufel   Hamburg

Contents

1 General Remarks on Compiler Theory

Programming languages are the main tools a computer scientist uses to work with computers. Only a few decades ago, in the beginning of computer programming, so-called *first generation languages* were used to make computers solve problems. Such languages are operating on the binary machine code level, which is a sequence of 0s and 1s that instruct the computer to perform actions. Thus programming was very difficult and troublesome. A small step forward was done by the introduction of programming in octal or hexadecimal code.

Machine code was replaced by *second generation languages*, i.e. *assembly languages*. These languages allowed mnemonic abbreviations as symbolic names and the abstraction has changed from the flip-flop level to the register level. First steps towards program structuring were recognizable, although the term "structured programming" cannot be used for assembler programs. The main disadvantage of the usage of assembly languages is that programs are still machine dependent and, in general, only readable by the authors.

Assembler languages were replaced by *third generation languages* or so-called *high level languages*. These languages allow control structures which are based on logical data objects [TEUF 91]: Variables of a specific type. They provide a level of abstraction allowing machine-independent specification of data, functions or processes, and their control. Typical representatives of third generation languages are:

- ALGOL 60,

- PASCAL,

- C, or

- MODULA-2.

The relations between these three levels of programming languages are shown in Figure 1.1.

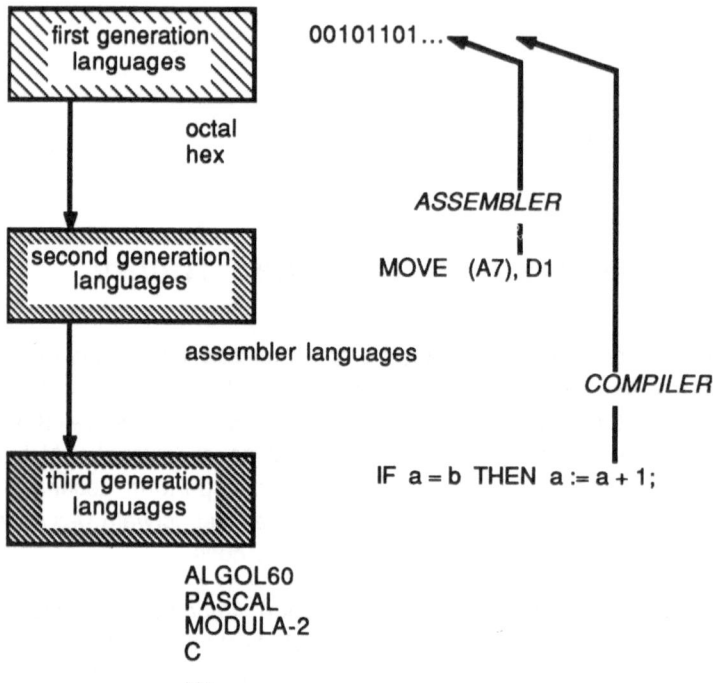

Fig. 1.1.   From low level to high level languages

The design of programs for solving complex problems is much easier using high level languages, because less knowledge about the computer's internal structure is necessary - but it is an obvious fact that the computer still just understands machine code. Thus, before a computer can execute high-level language programs, they must be translated into machine code. This process is called *compilation* and the corresponding tool is called a *compiler* (see Figure 1.2). Hence, compilers are fundamental to computing, not only at present but also in the future.

A compiler's input is the *source code*, i.e. the program written in a high-level language. The compiler performs some checks, and analyzes this input as described briefly later in this Chapter and in more detail in the following Chapters. The output of the compiler is the so-called *object code*, i.e. the machine instructions or machine code. As we will see later, different forms of machine code exist; the simplest differentiation between these codes is an absolute and relocatable code.

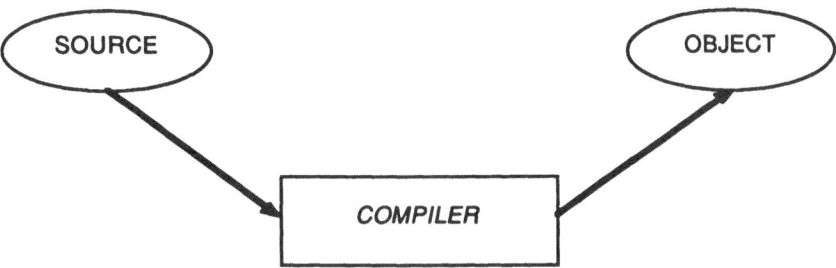

Fig. 1.2. The concept of compilation

1.1 Types of Compilation Systems

Generally, compilation systems translate some kind of source code into object code. This is a very simplified view of compilation systems, reality is a bit more complex than that. But even on this simple level, a classification of compilation systems can be found. According to the different kinds of codes and different kinds of functioning, we distinguish between different types of compilation systems:

- *Assembler*: An assembly language is a more understandable form of machine code. It is the first step to a mnemonic program representation. Assemblers translate programs which are written in an assembly language (characterized by the usage of mnemonics representing machine operations and probably symbolic addresses) into machine code. Some of the ideas which can be found in modern compiler theory have already been established in assemblers (e.g. the usage of symbol tables).

- *Compiler*: Compilers translate programs which are written in a high-level language into a so-called intermediary code or into machine code. The intermediary code could be, for example, an assembly language or some other form of intermediary representation as described in Chapter 5.
  One can often find the attribute *optimizing* in combination with *compiler*, which is in general a deception, since the generation of optimal code is an NP-complete problem. Generally speaking, an optimizing compiler is designed to generate efficient machine code, i.e. the best possible but not necessarily optimal code. Usually, this is achieved by an increase in the compiler's complexity and the compilation time, but results probably in

less object code and shorter execution times. Certain optimizing techniques are described in Chapter 7.

- *Interpreter*: An interpreter does not generate object code. Instead, each statement of the source code is directly analyzed and executed. Since no machine code is generated, interpreters are in some form machine independent. In general, an interpreter must just be recompiled to run on another target hardware.

- *Preprocessor*: The task of a preprocessor could be, for example, macro substitution, file inclusion, or language extension. For example, the preprocessor of a C-compiler interprets lines of a C-program beginning with #. A control line of the form

```
#include  <stdio.h>
```

causes the replacement of that line by the entire content of the file stdio.h.

In this text, we do neither consider assemblers or interpreters, nor preprocessors, but all the different phases of the compilation process.

1.2   Compiler Environments

Compilers often produce, as a result of the semantic analysis, some form of *intermediary representation* of the source code. Today, it becomes common that on workstation or mainframe environments all the compilers for the different languages generate the same intermediary code which then by a so-called code generator is transformed to the actual object code. This causes an important advantage. We have just to replace a single code generator - instead of all compilers - if the operating system or something else has changed. The generation of an intermediary code makes compilers more portable, since all their machine independent parts (as they will be described in Chapters 3 through 6) need not to be changed for a new target hardware. Furthermore, a compiler's maintenance will be simplified according to the above-mentioned reasons.

Figure 1.3 shows a simple example of a PASCAL procedure which is translated into M68000 assembly code - the intermediary code, for example. The according hexadecimal code is also shown.

Normally, programs are not as simple as shown in Figure 1.3. The source code of complex program systems usually consists of several modules or imports at least some standard functions from different libraries - especially when using programming languages like MODULA-2. Therefore, it will be necessary to combine the codes of different sources to a single executable object. We call this process *linkage* and the corresponding tool is called *linker*. Figure 1.4 shows the main elements of a system which transforms a source code into an executable program.

```
SOURCE              INTERMEDIARY           HEXADECIMAL
                    CODE                   CODE
_____

procedure add_int   * SECTION 9 defines    00000000 222F 0004
   (i, j, integer;  * the code section     00000004 202F 0008
   var sum integer);* SECTION 14 defines   00000008 206F 000C
                    * the data section     0000000C D081
begin               * A7: stack pointer    0000000E 2080
   sum := i + j;    *                      00000010 4E75
end;                  SECTION 9
                      XDEF    .add_int
                    .add_int:
                      MOVE.L 4(A7),D1
                      MOVE.L 8(A7),D0
                      MOVE.L 12(A7),A0
                      ADD.L  D1,D0
                      MOVE.L D0,(A0)
                      RTS
                    *
                      SECTION 14
                    * allocations for add_int
                    * 4(A7)   .i
                    * 8(A7)   .j
                    * 12(A7) .sum
```

Fig. 1.3.   From source to object via intermediary code

Here it should be noted that in terms of a modern compiler environment, Figure 1.4 is not complete. Modern compiler environments should support not only the compilation process, but the whole development of a program. This means that such an environment should be completed by

- an intelligent syntax-driven editing system (probably based on a problem specification tool), as well as

- a symbolic debugging system.

However, the fundamental techniques in compilers are the same, no matter how convenient or inconvenient the environment will be. Since we are just interested in those fundamental techniques, we put no emphasis on marginal questions like editing and debugging systems.

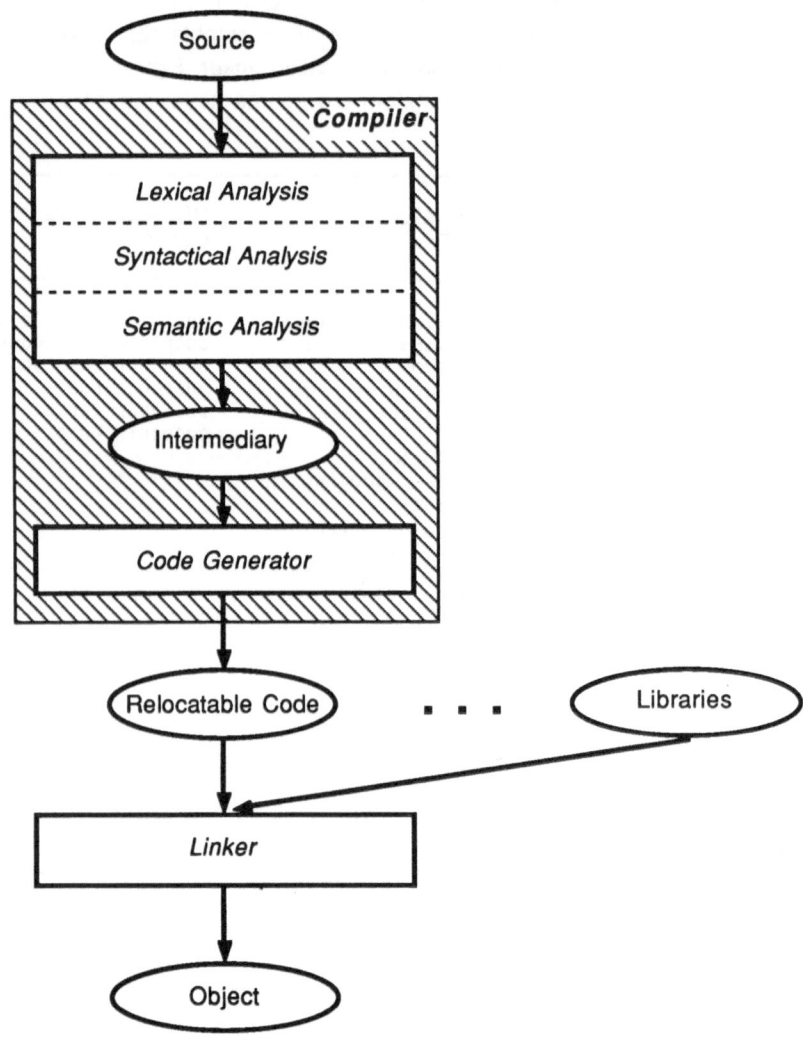

Fig. 1.4.   A general compiler environment

1.3   Analysis and Synthesis

Compiling a program means analyzing and synthesizing that program, i.e.
determining the structure and meaning of a source code and translating that source
code into an equivalent machine code. The major tasks or phases of a compiler
are:

- Lexical Analysis (Scanning),

- Syntax Analysis,

- Semantic Analysis, and

- Code Generation.

A program can be considered as a stream of characters which is the input to the *lexical analysis*. The task of the lexical analysis is the recognition of tokens within that stream, i.e. the transformation of a character stream onto a token stream. (As in natural language texts we can distinguish between *words* and *tokens*: the number of words determine the program's vocabulary size, while the number of tokens determine the length of the program). For example, the statement

```
i := 10;
```

will result in the following:

- The identifier i.

- The assignment symbol :=.

- The number 10.

- The delimiter symbol ; (semi-colon).

The recognized identifiers or names are organized in a so-called *symbol table*, which is a data structure containing a record with attribute fields for each name. The content of the symbol table is completed by lexical and syntactical analysis and will be used for semantic analysis and code generation.

The next step is called *syntax analysis*. The word syntax means "the structure of the word order in a sentence" [BRIN 85]. Other terms for syntax analysis are *hierarchical analysis* or *parsing*. The task of the syntactical analysis is to check whether the symbols occur in the right order (i.e. to check whether a source was designed according to the syntax of the considered programming language) and to combine the symbols of the source code in grammatical units. In this phase we will find syntactical errors like

```
h + x := x * y .
```

In general, the grammatical units are organized and represented using *parse trees* or *syntax trees*. Figure 1.5 shows such a parse tree for the following statement:

```
h := x + y - x * y .
```

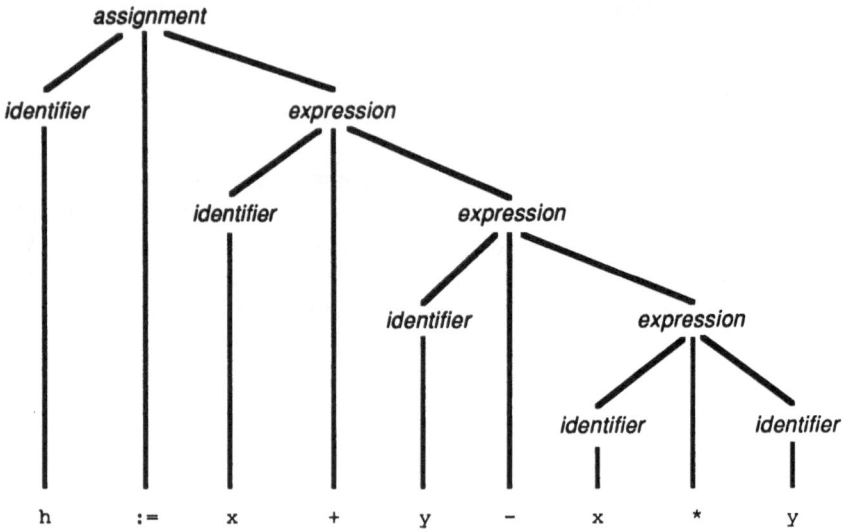

Fig. 1.5.   A parse tree

The syntax analysis is followed by the *semantic* and *type analysis*. The semantic analysis is harder to do than the syntax analysis, because we have to consider the meaning of a given grammatical unit, i.e. we have to interpret such a unit. This can be done by translating the input into some form of intermediary representation. For example, if we had never defined the variable h in Figure 1.5, the assignment statement would be meaningless. Analogously, the assignment of a boolean variable to a real variable would be meaningless, too. Such inconsistencies will be recognized by type analysis.

The object code is generated in the last compilation phase: the *code generator*. In this phase, the intermediary code is transformed into machine code and the necessary storage will be determined. Obviously, this is the only phase which depends on the used hardware, because different computers have, in general, different instruction sets.

2 Formal Aspects

Compilers translate languages which usually consist of syntactical elements that can easily be described in a formal way. Therefore, compilers cannot be treated without considering formal aspects of language definition. However, the theory of formal languages is an independent discipline and we will introduce only as much formalism as we think is necessary to understand compilers. This Chapter may then be thought of as the definition module for this text. Terminology for grammars and languages, as well as the basic analyzing techniques are introduced. Finally, the definition of the programming language PL/0 is given - this language will be used in the following Chapters to explain particular methods.

Before starting with meta-languages and formal languages let us define some of the most important elements of languages.

Definitions

- *Alphabet*: An alphabet is an arbitrary but finite set of *symbols*.
  For example, machine code is based on the binary alphabet $A_1 = \{0, 1\}$; other examples are $A_2 = \{0, 1, 2, 3, 4, 5, 6, 7, 8, 9\}$, $A_3 = \{+, -, *, /\}$ etc.

- *Symbols*: The elements of the vocabulary (alphabet) of a formal language are called symbols, while for natural languages we call them *words*.

- *Token*: Multiple occurrences of symbols (or words) are called tokens.

- *Sentence*: A sequence of symbols is called a sentence.

- *Grammar (Syntax)*: The grammar or the syntax of a language defines whether an arbitrary sequence of symbols is correct, i.e. is a meaningful sentence. We will say that a correct sentence will be accepted by the language.

- *String*: A (finite) sequence of elements of a certain set (alphabet) will be called a string. Analogously to the empty set in set theory we can consider an empty string ε. The *empty string ε* is a string which contains no symbols.
  The sequence 0011 is an example of a string of the alphabet A_1.

- *Production*: Rules for string substitution are called productions. The symbols $\rightarrow$ and ::= are widely used to represent productions.
  For example, the rule (production) $s \rightarrow a\, b$ (or $s ::= a\, b$) means that s can be substituted by $a\, b$, or s is defined as $a\, b$.

- *Terminal symbols*: The symbols which actually occur in a sentence are called terminal symbols. They will never occur on the left side of a production. Terminal symbols must be valid symbols of the language. The symbols **begin**, **end**, **if**, **then**, **else** are an example for terminal symbols belonging to the grammar which describes PASCAL.
  T indicates the set of terminal symbols, while T^* indicates the set of all possible strings over T.

- *Nonterminal symbols*: Nonterminal symbols must be defined by other productions (or BNF-rules, see 2.1), i.e. they occur also on the left side of productions. Nonterminal symbols are syntactical variables.
  N indicates the set of nonterminal symbols, while N^* indicates the set of all possible strings over N.

- *Vocabulary = Alphabet*: Like natural languages, formal languages are based on a specific vocabulary, i.e. the elements of the language. The vocabulary of a formal language is the union of the terminal and nonterminal symbols.
  $V = N \cup T$ indicates the vocabulary, while V^* indicates the set of all possible strings over V.

The * in these definitions indicates the *closure* of a certain set. We will find a similar usage of this operator for productions.

2.1   Backus-Naur Form (BNF)

To be able to compile a program which is written in a specific programming language, we have to know the definition of that programming language. Defining a programming language means describing the syntax and semantics of that language. We can specify the syntax of a programming language - a formal language - using the so-called *Backus-Naur form* (BNF). BNF was introduced for defining the syntactical structure of the programming language ALGOL60 (cf. [NAUR 63]).

Table 2.1. BNF-notation

symbol	meaning
→	"is defined as"
.	end of a definition
|	"or", alternative
[x]	one or no occurrence of x
{ x }	an arbitrary occurrence of x (0, 1, 2, ...)
(x | y)	selection (x or y)

The Backus-Naur form is a so-called *meta-language*, i.e. a language which is used to describe other languages. There exist some dialects of the BNF-notation. Table 2.1 shows some usual (meta-) symbols of the BNF. Using this notation and the terminal symbols

$$T \quad = \quad \{ +, -, 0, 1, 2, 3, 4, 5, 6, 7, 8, 9 \}$$

as well as the nonterminal symbols

$$N \quad = \quad \{ \textit{int, unsigned\_int, digit} \}$$

we can define integers by the following BNF-rules (productions):

int	→	[+ | -] *unsigned_int* .
unsigned_int	→	*digit* | *unsigned_int digit* .
digit	→	0 | 1 | 2 | 3 | 4 | 5 | 6 | 7 | 8 | 9 .

The first rule defines an integer as an unsigned integer with a leading sign. This sign can be absent, or "+", or "-". The second rule shows that BNF allows recursive definitions.

A formal description of a language is given, if a finite number of BNF-rules exists, allowing the derivation of any sentence of the language. In this respect, the finite set of rules given above are a formal description of the infinite set of integers.

2.2 Formal Languages

In this section we will give a brief introduction to formal languages making known those terms and rules which are important to compiler theory. The field of formal languages is a wide area and an independent field of research. A fundamental introduction to this topic would be beyond the scope of this text. Therefore, for a more detailed description on the theory of formal languages we refer to books like [KUIC 86] or [SALO 73], for example.

The BNF is a meta-language which is often used to define the syntactical structure of a programming language. But it could also be used to define English sentences. We will use this example to explain some rules and terminology of formal languages, thereby giving a brief introduction into the ideas of Noam Chomsky who tried to formalize natural languages. For example, an English sentence (S) consists of a "noun phrase" (NP) followed by a "verb phrase" (VP). In BNF this will be described as

     S   →   NP   VP.

In this production NP and VP are *nonterminal symbols*.

A language which accepts the sentence

      the man took the ball

could be defined by the following productions:

     S   →   NP VP.
     NP →   T   N.
     T   →   the.
     N   →   man | ball | book.
     VP →   V NP.
     V   →   took | bought.

Hence, the defined language consists of the following 18 sentences (obviously, this language considers the English syntax, but is far away from every day English consisting of syntax and semantics):

the man took the man	the man took the ball
the man took the book	the man bought the man
the man bought the ball	the man bought the book
the ball took the man	the ball took the ball
the ball took the book	the ball bought the man
the ball bought the ball	the ball bought the book
the book took the man	the book took the ball
the book took the book	the book bought the man
the book bought the ball	the book bought the book

Such a complete syntactical description of a language will be called a *grammar*. A grammar consists of a set of rules where each nonterminal symbol is defined. One of the nonterminal symbols is marked as a *start symbol* and, therefore, is the starting point of the grammar. For example, such a start symbol could be "MODULE" or "PROGRAM" when considering the programming languages MODULA-2 or PASCAL, respectively.

A grammar G will be defined as a 4-tuple G (T, N, P, S), where

- T is the set of terminal symbols,

- N is the set of nonterminal symbols,

- P is the set of productions,

- $S \in N$ is the start symbol.

A (*formal*) *language* L will be characterized with reference to a grammar G:

$$L\,(G)\ =\quad L\,(T, N, P, S).$$

We say that a string β could be *directly derived* from a string α

$$\alpha \quad \rightarrow \quad \beta$$

if there exists just one production to produce β from α, e.g.

$$\alpha \quad = \quad \alpha_1 \alpha_2 \alpha_3$$

$$\beta \quad = \quad \alpha_1 \beta_2 \alpha_3$$

and there exists the production

$$\alpha_2 \quad \rightarrow \quad \beta_2.$$

We say that a string α_n can be *derived* from a string α_0 if and only if a sequence of strings $\alpha_0, \alpha_1, \alpha_2, \ldots, \alpha_{n-1}$ exists, so that each α_i can be directly derived by α_{i-1} ($i = 1, 2, \ldots, n$):

$$\alpha_0 \quad \rightarrow \quad \alpha_1 \quad \rightarrow \quad \alpha_2 \quad \rightarrow \quad \ldots \quad \rightarrow \quad \alpha_{n-1} \quad \rightarrow \quad \alpha_n$$

A sequence of such productions will be abbreviated with $\rightarrow^*$:

$$\alpha_0 \quad \rightarrow^* \quad \alpha_n \quad \equiv \quad (\alpha_{i-1} \quad \rightarrow \quad \alpha_i \ , \ i = 1, 2, \ldots, n)$$

and $\rightarrow^*$ is said to be the *reflexive transitive closure* of $\rightarrow$. For example, the sentence

the man bought the book

can be derived by the following sequence of productions:

S	$\rightarrow$	NP		VP		
	$\rightarrow$	T	N	VP		
	$\rightarrow$	the	N	VP		
	$\rightarrow$	the	man	VP		
	$\rightarrow$	the	man	V	NP	
	$\rightarrow$	the	man	bought	NP	
	$\rightarrow$	the	man	bought	T	N
	$\rightarrow$	the	man	bought	the	N
	$\rightarrow$	the	man	bought	the	book

Thus, if we abbreviate

the man bought the book $\equiv$ tmbtb ,

it holds that

S $\rightarrow^*$ tmbtb ,

and tmbtb will be accepted by the language which is based on the set of productions given above, tmbtb $\in$ L , because tmbtb $\in$ T^*.

Now, we can define a language L (G) as the set of all strings of terminal symbols which can be derived from the start symbol S :

$$L \quad = \quad \{ \sigma \mid S \rightarrow^* \sigma \text{ and } \sigma \in T^* \} .$$

Properties and Definitions

Considering the derivation process we can find two important strategies: *leftmost derivations* and *rightmost derivations*. A derivation is called leftmost (rightmost) if it is always the leftmost (rightmost) nonterminal that is replaced. We will need this definition to understand the functioning of several parsing methods (cf. Chapter 4). An example for left- and rightmost derivations will be given later in this section.

A BNF-rule

$$v \quad \rightarrow \quad \sigma$$

specifies that a (single) nonterminal symbol $v \in N$ can be replaced by $\sigma \in (N \cup T)^*$ regardless of the context in which v occurs. Such productions will be called *context-free*.

According to N. Chomsky we call a grammar and the corresponding language context-free if and only if it can be defined with a set of context-free productions. Context-free grammars are very important in the theory of programming languages, since the languages they define are, in general, simple in their structure. Parsing techniques are usually based on context-free grammars.

A context-free grammar will be called *unambiguous* if and only if there exists just one rightmost (leftmost) derivation and therefore one parse tree (i.e. the sequence of derivations represented as a tree structure) for each sentence that can be derived by the productions of the grammar. Otherwise, it will be called *ambiguous*. We will give a few examples on ambiguity later in this Chapter, when we have introduced parse trees.

A sentence of an ambiguous grammar can have more than one parse tree and therefore, it can have more than one meaning. Thus, ambiguous grammars are not very useful for the analysis and the definition of programming languages. They are hard to handle and we normally try to transform them into unambiguous ones. It should be noted that it is an undecidable problem to determine whether a given grammar is ambiguous or not. As we will see later, there exist some conditions which - if fulfilled - are sufficient to say that a certain grammar is unambiguous. But these conditions are not necessary. This means that a grammar which does not fulfil these conditions cannot be said to be ambiguous (or even unambiguous).

A grammar G (T, N, P, S) is said to be *left-linear*, if each production P is of the form

$$A \rightarrow Ba \quad \text{or} \quad A \rightarrow a \, ,$$

where A and B are in N and a is in T^*.

G (T, N, P, S) is called *right-linear*, if each production P is of the form

$$A \rightarrow aB \qquad \text{or} \qquad A \rightarrow a \,,$$

where A and B are in N and a is in T^*. Right-linear grammars G (T, N, P, S) are often referred to as *regular* (or *finite-state*).

In general, the syntax of a programming language cannot be expressed by a regular grammar but certain elements of a language, such as names or numbers, are preferably described by regular grammars. Thus, lexical analysis as shown in Chapter 3 will be based on a regular grammar.

A nonterminal X ∈ N in a context-free grammar G (T, N, P, S) is said to be *recursive* if

$$X \rightarrow^* \alpha X \beta$$

for some α and β. X is said to be *left-recursive* (*right-recursive*) if $\alpha = \varepsilon$ ($\beta = \varepsilon$). A grammar with at least one left- (right-) recursive nonterminal X is said to be left- (right-) recursive, and it is said to be recursive if all nonterminals (except possibly the start symbol) are recursive. Some of the parsing algorithms do not work with left-recursive grammars, since such grammars bear the risk of infinite loops.

The inversion of a derivation is called *reduction*. Instead of *β can be (directly) derived from α* ($\alpha \rightarrow \beta$), it is also possible to say that *β can be (directly) reduced to α* ($\beta \leftarrow \alpha$). These forms are equivalent:

$$\alpha \rightarrow \beta \qquad \equiv \qquad \beta \leftarrow \alpha$$
$$\alpha \rightarrow^* \beta \qquad \equiv \qquad \beta \,^*\!\!\leftarrow \alpha$$

Obviously, the inversion of a leftmost derivation is a *rightmost reduction* and the inversion of a rightmost derivation is a *leftmost reduction*.

Hierarchy of Grammars

Grammars are classified according to their complexity. This classification - often referred to as *Chomsky-Hierarchy* - is given by increasing the restrictions on the form of the productions (cf. Figure 2.1).

Type 0 grammars are *no-restriction grammars*, i.e. there are neither restrictions for the left side nor for the right side of the productions. Such general grammars are of no relevance for today's programming languages. Writing a parser for a type 0 grammar would be a very hard task. The form of the productions of type 1 grammars implies that replacements can only be done in a certain context, i.e. these are *context-sensitive grammars*. In contrast to that, type 2 grammars are *context-free grammars*, while the left- and right-linear type 3 grammars are *regular grammars*. Clearly, a grammar of type i + 1 is also of type i, i = 0, 1, 2.

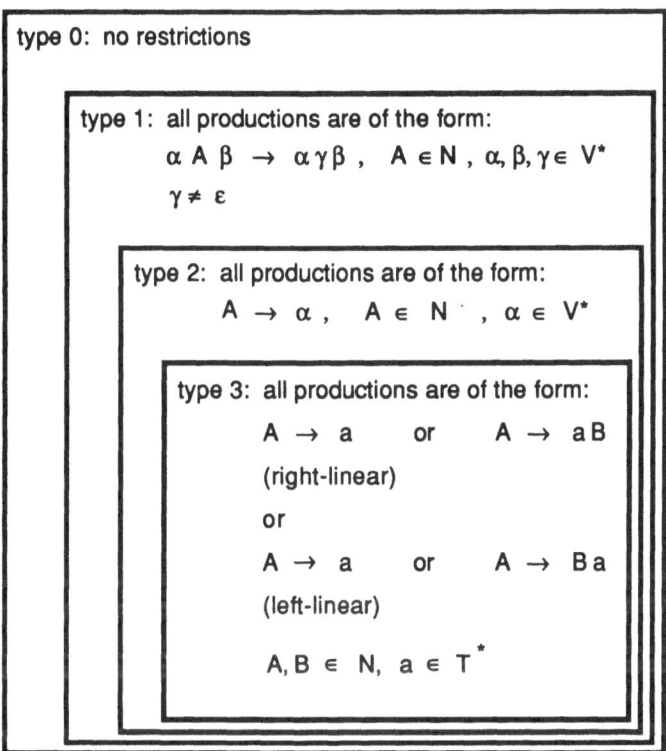

type 0: no restrictions

type 1: all productions are of the form:

$$\alpha\, A\, \beta\ \rightarrow\ \alpha\,\gamma\,\beta\ ,\quad A \in N\ ,\ \alpha, \beta, \gamma \in V^*$$
$$\gamma \neq \varepsilon$$

type 2: all productions are of the form:

$$A\ \rightarrow\ \alpha\ ,\quad A \in N\ ,\ \alpha \in V^*$$

type 3: all productions are of the form:

$$A\ \rightarrow\ a\qquad \text{or}\qquad A\ \rightarrow\ a\,B$$
(right-linear)
or
$$A\ \rightarrow\ a\qquad \text{or}\qquad A\ \rightarrow\ B\,a$$
(left-linear)

$$A, B \in N,\ a \in T^*$$

Fig. 2.1.   Chomsky-Hierarchy

For i = 0, 1, 2, 3, we call a language of type i, if it is generated by a grammar of type i, i.e. a context-free grammar generates a context-free language, a regular grammar generates a regular language and so on. From the compiler writer's view, type 2 and type 3 grammars are the most important. While context-free grammars define the syntax of declarations, statements, and expressions, etc. (i.e. the structure of a program), the regular grammars define the syntax of identifiers, numbers, strings, and other basic symbols of the language. Thus, context-free grammars can normally be found in syntactical analysis, while regular grammars are used as a basis for lexical analysis.

For example, in most programming languages there are a number of pairs of brackets which have to be matched, such as

begin   end, repeat   until, if   fi, ( ), [ ].

Of course, there must be the appropriate closing bracket for each opening bracket. Minsky showed that such strings of opening and closing brackets cannot be generated by regular grammars [MINS 67]. But the following context-free grammar is an example for the generation of such strings of brackets:

T   =   { **begin, end** }
N   =   { A }
P   =   { A   →   **begin** A **end** A | ε }
S   =   { A }

This grammar produces for each **begin** the according **end**, e.g.

begin begin begin   end end end   begin   end

is a sentence of that language.

However, typical programming languages consist of properties which cannot be expressed by means of context-free grammars (or even regular grammars). For example, an assignment statement x := y * x; may only be legal (and meaningful) if x and y are already declared and are of compatible types. Such context-sensitive problems are normally handled using symbol tables.

Parse Trees

Up to now, we have shown that a grammar can be used to generate sentences of a specific language. However, a compiler does not have to generate programs but to check strings of symbols to determine whether they belong to the language, i.e. to find how a sequence of symbols might be derived from the start symbol using the productions of the grammar and to display the derivation (or to show that the sentence cannot be derived from the start symbol). This problem is known as the *parsing problem*.

The derivation process can be illustrated by a tree as shown below. To exemplify this, we define a grammar G_0 (T_0, N_0, P_0, S_0) which accepts arithmetic expressions like x + y - x * y.

T_0 =   { x, y, +, -, *, /, (,) }
N_0 =   { EXPR, TERM, FACTOR }

$$P_0 \;=\; \{\, \text{EXPR} \;\rightarrow\; \text{TERM} \mid \text{EXPR} + \text{TERM} \mid \text{EXPR} - \text{TERM}$$

$$\text{TERM} \;\rightarrow\; \text{FACTOR} \mid \text{TERM} * \text{FACTOR} \mid \text{TERM} / \text{FACTOR}$$

$$\text{FACTOR} \;\rightarrow\; x \mid y \mid (\text{EXPR}) \,\}$$

$$S_0 \;=\; \{\, \text{EXPR} \,\}$$

We see that each expression is a sequence of terms which are separated by "+" or "-". Figure 2.2 shows the parse tree for the expression $x + y - x * y$. It represents graphically the derivation of a sentence of the language according to the grammar G_0 (T_0, N_0, P_0, S_0).

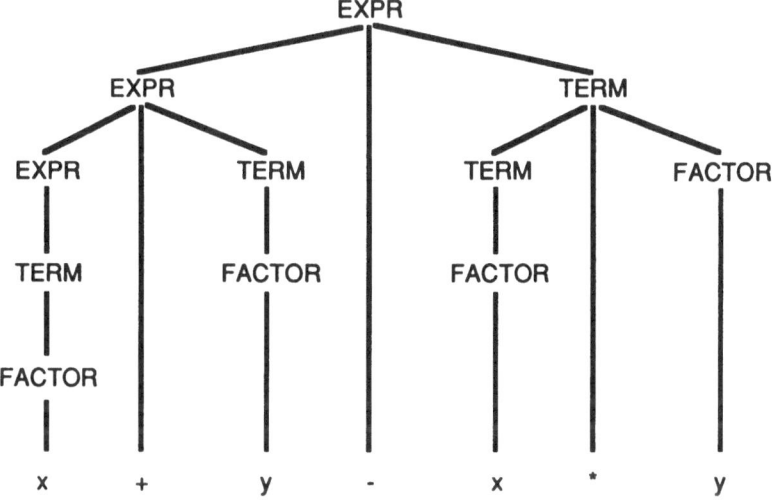

Fig. 2.2.   Parse tree for the expression $x + y - x * y$

We can also consider the leftmost derivation of $x + y - x * y$:

EXPR	$\rightarrow$	EXPR - TERM
	$\rightarrow$	EXPR + TERM - TERM
	$\rightarrow$	TERM + TERM - TERM
	$\rightarrow$	FACTOR + TERM - TERM
	$\rightarrow$	x + TERM - TERM
	$\rightarrow$	x + FACTOR - TERM
	$\rightarrow$	x + y - TERM
	$\rightarrow$	x + y - TERM * FACTOR
	$\rightarrow$	x + y - FACTOR * FACTOR
	$\rightarrow$	x + y - x * FACTOR
	$\rightarrow$	x + y - x * y

The rightmost derivation is:

$$
\begin{array}{lll}
\text{EXPR} & \rightarrow & \text{EXPR - TERM} \\
 & \rightarrow & \text{EXPR - TERM * FACTOR} \\
 & \rightarrow & \text{EXPR - TERM * y} \\
 & \rightarrow & \text{EXPR - FACTOR * y} \\
 & \rightarrow & \text{EXPR - x * y} \\
 & \rightarrow & \text{EXPR + TERM - x * y} \\
 & \rightarrow & \text{EXPR + FACTOR - x * y} \\
 & \rightarrow & \text{EXPR + y - x * y} \\
 & \rightarrow & \text{TERM + y - x * y} \\
 & \rightarrow & \text{FACTOR + y - x * y} \\
 & \rightarrow & \text{x + y - x * y}
\end{array}
$$

Considering a context-free grammar, we can state the following properties of a parse tree (cf. [AHOS 86]):

- The root is marked by the start symbol.

- Each leaf is marked by a terminal symbol or with ε.

- Each node is marked by a nonterminal symbol.

The process of generating a parse tree for a given expression will be called *syntax analysis* or *parsing*.

Now, that we have introduced parse trees, we can once more have a look at ambiguous and unambiguous grammars. Considering the language which is generated by grammar G_0, we can find at least two other grammars which generate the same language, i.e.:

$$
\begin{array}{lll}
T_0 & = & \{ x, y, +, -, *, /, (,) \} \\
N'_0 & = & \{ \text{EXPR, OP} \} \\
P'_0 & = & \{ \text{EXPR} \quad \rightarrow \quad \text{EXPR OP EXPR} \mid (\text{EXPR}) \mid x \mid y \\
 & & \quad \text{OP} \quad \rightarrow \quad + \mid - \mid * \mid / \} \\
S'_0 & = & \{ \text{EXPR} \}
\end{array}
$$

and

$$
\begin{array}{lll}
T''_0 & = & \{ x, y, +, -, *, /, (,) \} \\
N''_0 & = & \{ \text{EXPR} \} \\
P''_0 & = & \{ \text{EXPR} \quad \rightarrow \quad \text{EXPR + EXPR} \mid \text{EXPR - EXPR} \mid \\
 & & \qquad\qquad\qquad \text{EXPR * EXPR} \mid \text{EXPR / EXPR} \mid \\
 & & \qquad\qquad\qquad (\text{EXPR}) \mid x \mid y \} \\
S''_0 & = & \{ \text{EXPR} \}
\end{array}
$$

While grammar G_0 is unambiguous, both G'_0 and G''_0 are ambiguous, which can be seen by the different parse trees for the sentence $x + y - x * y$ given below. This example shows us also that there is no unique correspondence between a certain language and a grammar: Grammars with different sets of productions can generate the same language.

Grammar G'_0:

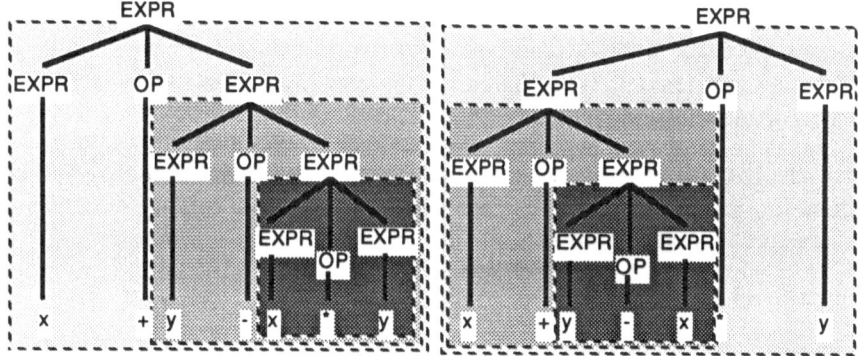

Grammar G''_0:

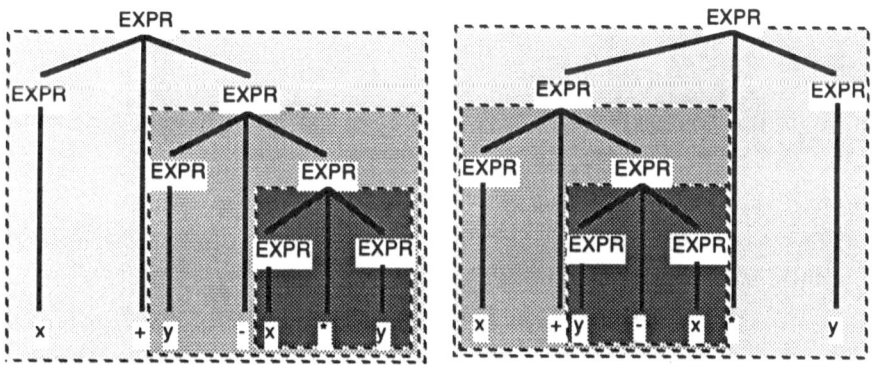

These examples of different parse trees for the same sentence of the language show explicitly the problem of ambiguous grammars: While in grammar G_0 only one interpretation of the given sentence is possible, both G'_0 and G''_0 allow more than one interpretation of the sentence. For example, the two parse trees belonging to grammar G'_0 imply the following two different interpretations:

$$(x + (y - (x * y))) \qquad \text{and} \qquad ((x + (y - x)) * y)$$

A similar interpretation holds for grammar G''_0. While grammar G_0 causes the usual ordering of arithmetic operators (cf. Figure 2.2), this is not true for G'_0 and G''_0, respectively. This should give us an understanding, why ambiguous grammars are problematic with respect to programming languages.

2.3   Analyzing Techniques

In the preceding section we have shown how a language can be defined formally by a grammar G (T, N, P, S), and how a specific sentence can be generated or derived. Now, the task of a compiler is not the generation of a sentence, but the *identification* of a sentence.

Syntax analysis or parsing is the process where we have to find the parse tree pertinent to a given sentence - according to the grammar of the programming language. In principle, there exist two methods for performing this analysis:

- *Top-down parsing*, and

- *Bottom-up parsing*.

The first method starts off from the root of the parse tree and works down to the leaves, while the second method works in reverse order, i.e. starts off from the leaves.

Top-down Parsing

We will explain this method by an example using the following simple grammar $G_1(T_1, N_1, P_1, S_1)$ which defines non-negative integers (NNI):

$$
\begin{aligned}
T_1 &= \quad \{\,0, 1, 2, 3, 4, 5, 6, 7, 8, 9\,\} \\
N_1 &= \quad \{\,\text{DIGIT, NNI}\,\} \\
P_1 &= \quad \{\,\text{NNI} \rightarrow \quad \text{DIGIT} \mid \text{NNI DIGIT} \\
&\qquad\quad \text{DIGIT} \rightarrow \quad 0 \mid 1 \mid 2 \mid 3 \mid 4 \mid 5 \mid 6 \mid 7 \mid 8 \mid 9\,\} \\
S_1 &= \quad \{\,\text{NNI}\,\}
\end{aligned}
$$

We want to analyze the sentence 123. At the beginning we just know the root of the tree and the sentence which has to be analyzed.

parse tree   *sentence*

NNI   1 2 3

In the first step we find the production NNI → NNI DIGIT and we get the beginning of the parse tree.

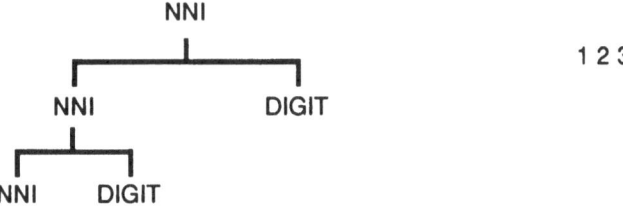

1 2 3

In the next step we will find the same production again.

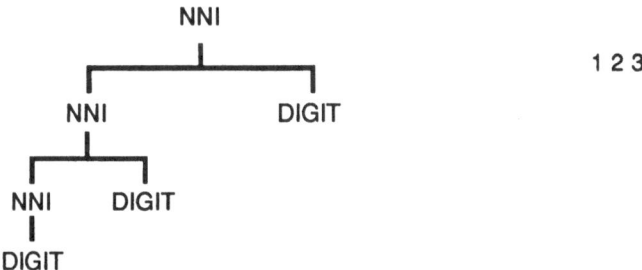

1 2 3

Then, we will find the production NNI → DIGIT which expands the parse tree to the following:

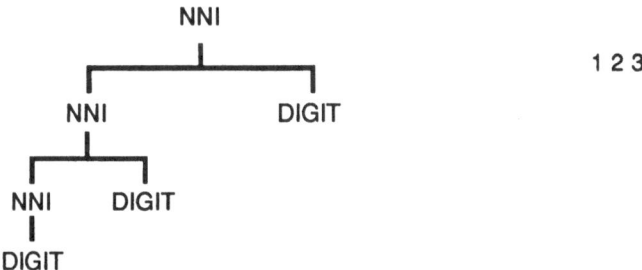

1 2 3

Now, we will find the production DIGIT → 1 which establishes the connection to the first element of the given sentence.

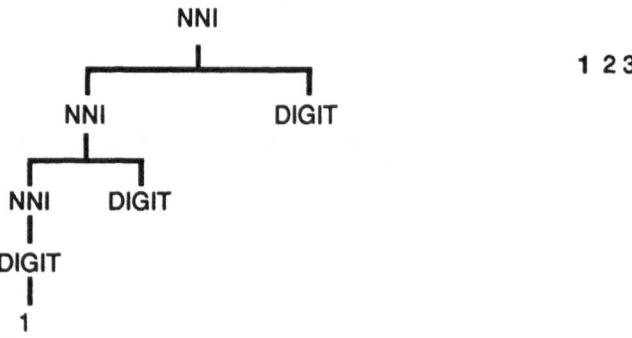

The production DIGIT → 2 establishes the connection to the second element of the sentence.

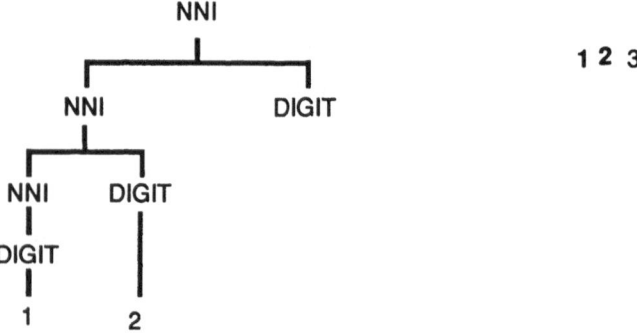

Finally the parse tree will be completed with the production DIGIT → 3.

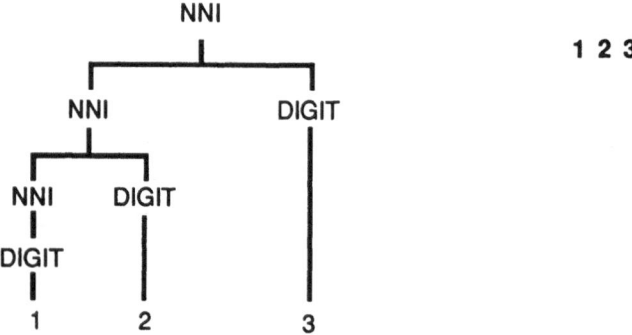

We see that the tree grows from the top to the bottom while the input sentence is read from left to right. Therefore, this method is called top-down parsing.

Bottom-up Parsing

We exemplify bottom-up parsing using grammar G_1 and sentence 123 once more. Again, we just know the root of the parse tree and the sentence which has to be analyzed. In the first step, we will find the reduction $1 \leftarrow$ DIGIT and we get the beginning of the parse tree.

In the second step we will find the reduction DIGIT $\leftarrow$ NNI and we will get the following parse tree:

The third step reduces the second element of the sentence using the reduction $2 \leftarrow$ DIGIT :

Then, the reduction NNI DIGIT $\leftarrow$ NNI is applied to continue the parse tree:

In the next step, the last element of the sentence will be reduced to digit: $3 \leftarrow$ DIGIT.

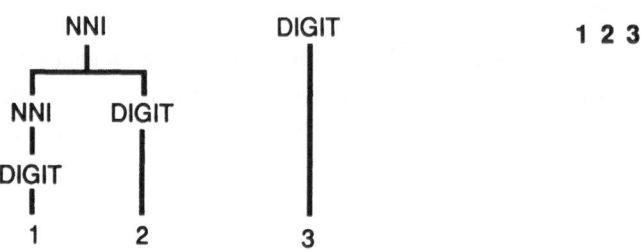

Finally, the parse tree is completed using the reduction NNI DIGIT ← NNI:

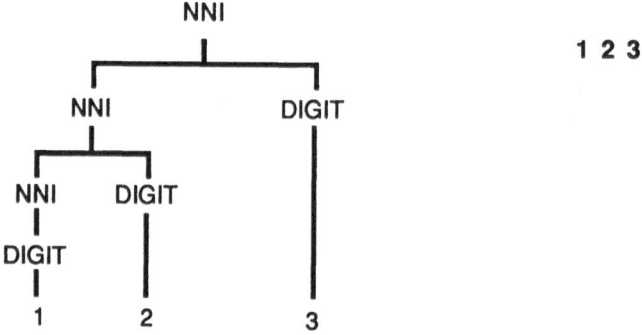

From this example, we can clearly see that we start off from the leaves of the parse tree and work to the root. Therefore, we call this method bottom-up parsing.

It is important to note that we came to the correct solution with both methods only because we had the given sentence in mind, i.e. we looked ahead. But without that look ahead technique, there would be several possibilities of making wrong decisions. For example, if we chose the production NNI → DIGIT in the first step of the top-down parse, we would not be able to get the parse tree for the sentence 123:

We would call this situation a *dead lock*. In order to solve such problems, so-called FIRST and FOLLOW sets will be defined (cf. Chapter 4). Let α be an arbitrary sequence of symbols. Then, FIRST(α) is the set of all terminal symbols that can be the prefix of any sentence that can be derived from α. Let N be a nonterminal symbol. Then, FOLLOW(N) is the set of all terminal symbols that can occur immediately to the right of N.

Using these two sets and some additional rules we can define the so-called LL(1) grammars allowing a top-down analysis with no dead locks. We will explain these techniques in more detail in Chapter 4.

2.4 Syntax Graphs

One way to represent the syntactical structure of a language is to use the BNF-notation. *Syntax graphs* are another (graphic) way to represent the syntax of a language. The graphic syntax representation makes a language definition easy to survey.

The language representation with syntax graphs is equivalent to the representation using BNF. According to [WIRT 86] we introduce six rules that allow the transformation of a BNF-notation into a syntax graph.

R1. Productions of the form

$$N \quad \rightarrow \quad \alpha_1 \mid \alpha_2 \mid \ldots \mid \alpha_n$$

will be represented by the following graph:

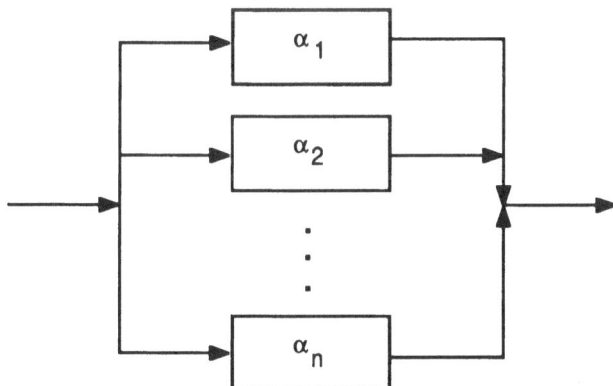

R2. Terms of the form

$$\alpha \quad = \quad a_1 \, a_2 \, \ldots \, a_n$$

will be represented by the following graph:

R3.   If an element has one or no occurrence, i.e.

> $[\alpha]$,

it will be represented by the following graph:

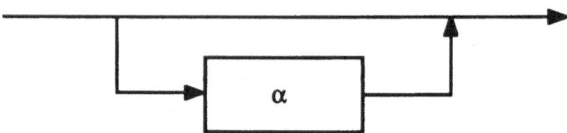

R4.   If an element is arbitrarily repeated (inclusive 0 times), i.e.

> $\{\alpha\}$,

it will be represented by the following graph:

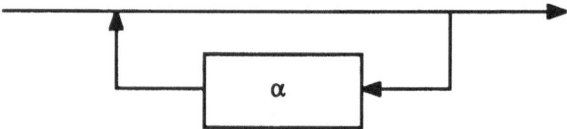

R5.   Nonterminal symbols N will be represented within a rectangle:

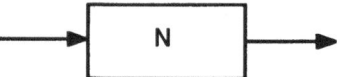

R6.   Terminal symbols t will be represented within a circle or an oval:

Obviously, a given sentence will be correct if and only if the elements of the sentence describe a correct path through the graphs. Using the rules R1 - R6 we can represent the grammar G_0 (T_0, N_0, P_0, S_0) by the following syntax graphs.

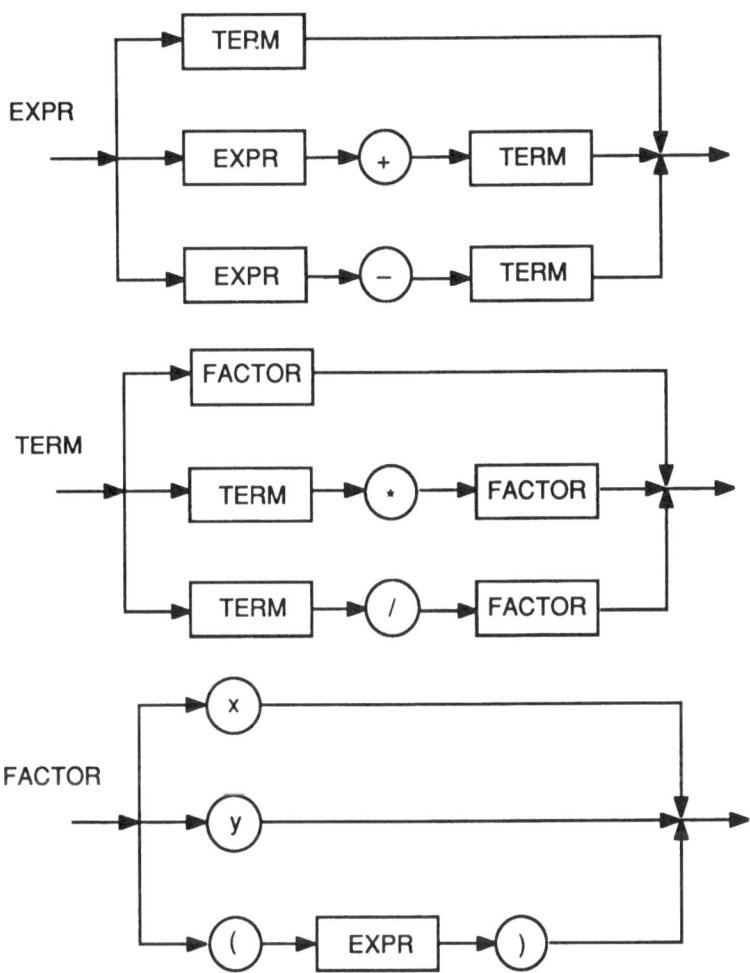

2.5   The Programming Language PL/0

The programming language PL/0 was defined by Niklaus Wirth [WIRT 86]. This language takes into account all major aspects of modern programming languages and it is as simple as it could be and as complex as it must be to demonstrate the principles and methods of compiling. Therefore, PL/0 will be used throughout this text to exemplify certain techniques. The definition of PL/0 is given by the following syntax graphs.

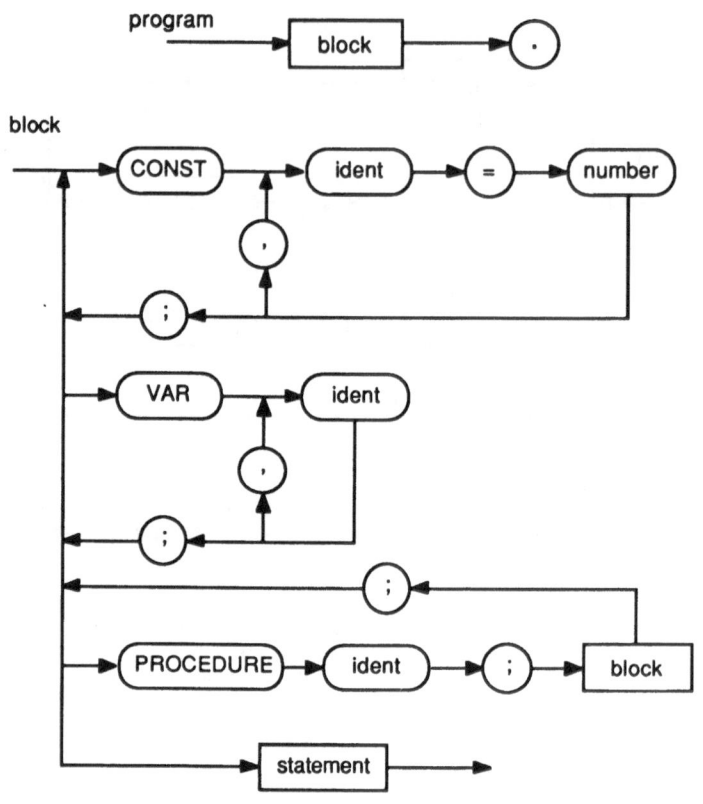

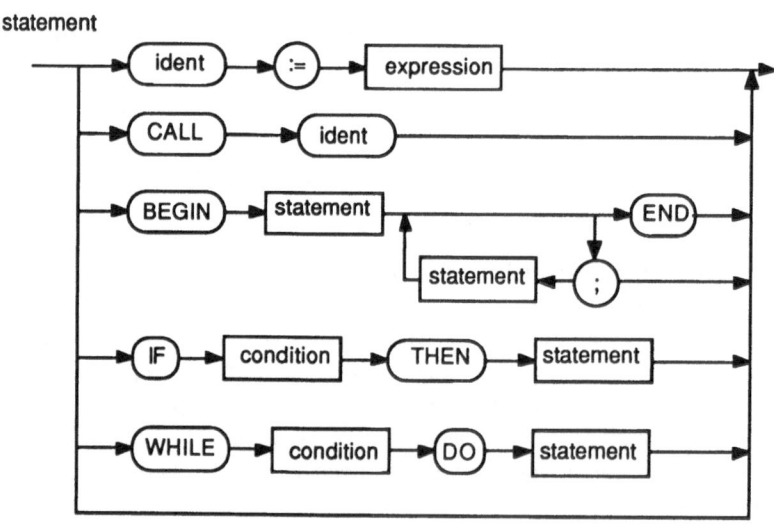

condition

expression

term

factor

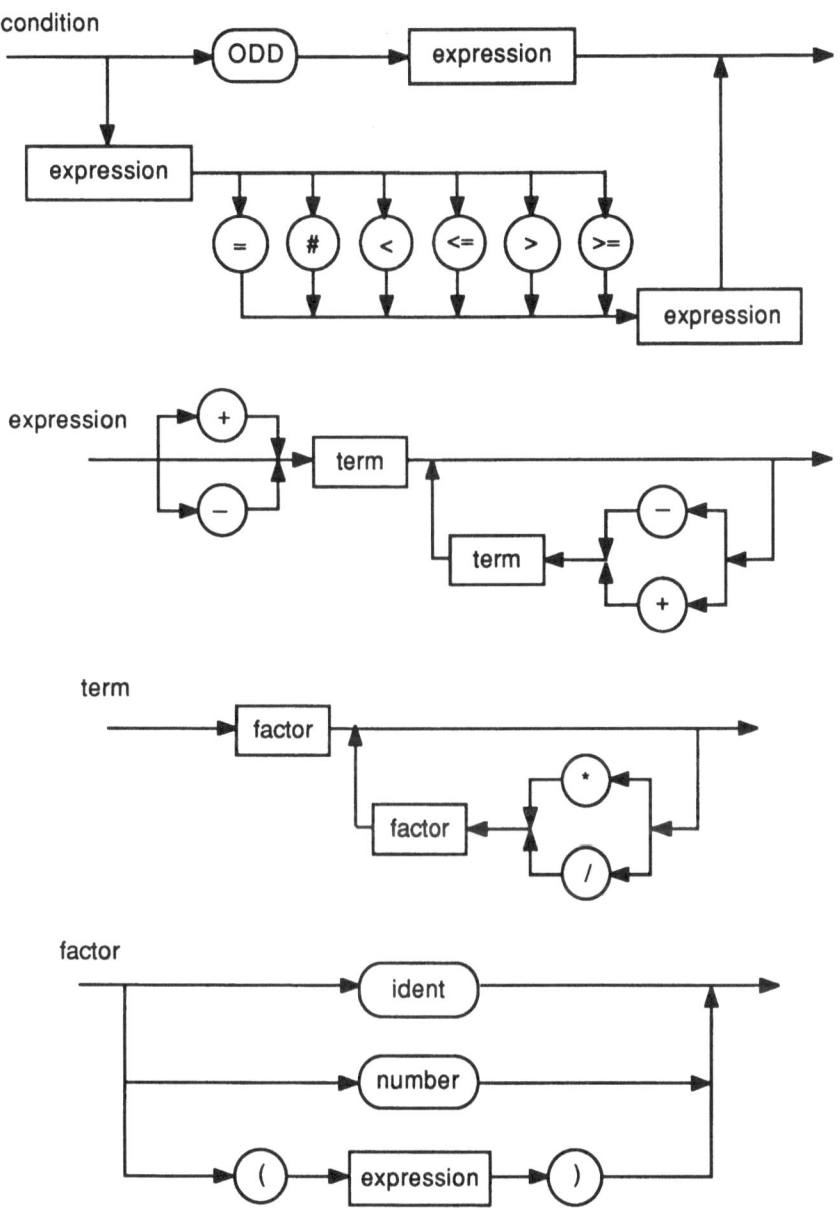

3 Lexical Analysis and Symbol Tables

At the beginning of the compilation process, the source code of a program is nothing else but a stream of characters. Thus, the task of the *lexical analysis* is to *recognize* symbols in this stream of characters and to provide these symbols in a more useful representation for syntax analysis. This process is shown in Figure 3.1.

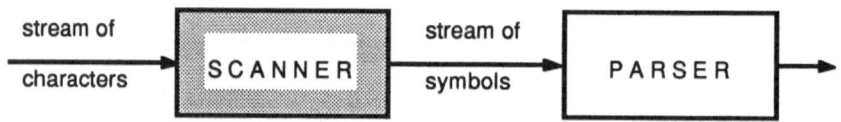

Fig. 3.1. Lexical analysis

The lexical analysis part of a compiler is called *scanner*. Typical functions of a scanner are:

- Skipping spaces, comments, etc.

- Recognizing identifiers and keywords.

- Recognizing constants and numerals.

- Generation of a compiler listing.

Before considering the scanner itself, we want to state some remarks on finite automata since such models are very convenient when describing the way symbols of formal languages (generated by regular grammars, cf. Chapter 2) should be analyzed.

3.1 Finite Automata

Scanners have to recognize tokens in a stream of characters and these tokens are elements of a regular language, i.e. they can be generated by a regular grammar. The following grammar G (T, N, P, S) is an example of a regular grammar

$$
\begin{array}{lll}
T & = & \{\,a, b\,\} \\
N & = & \{\,A, B, C\,\} \\
P & = & \{A & \rightarrow & A\,a \mid B\,a \\
  & & B & \rightarrow & C\,b \\
  & & C & \rightarrow & C\,a \mid a\,\} \\
S & = & \{\,A\,\}
\end{array}
$$

which generates the language

$$
L\,(G) \quad = \quad \{\,a^{m}\,b\,a^{n} \mid m, n \geq 1\,\} \ .
$$

The sentence *aaba* which belongs to L (G) has the following derivation:

$$
\begin{array}{lll}
A & \rightarrow & B\,a \\
  & \rightarrow & C\,b\,a \\
  & \rightarrow & C\,a\,b\,a \\
  & \rightarrow & a\,a\,b\,a
\end{array}
$$

Now, the recognition process reads a sentence from left to right and accepts that sentence as an element of the language if it can be reduced to the start symbol of the grammar. This is shown in Figure 3.2 for the sentence *aaabaa*.

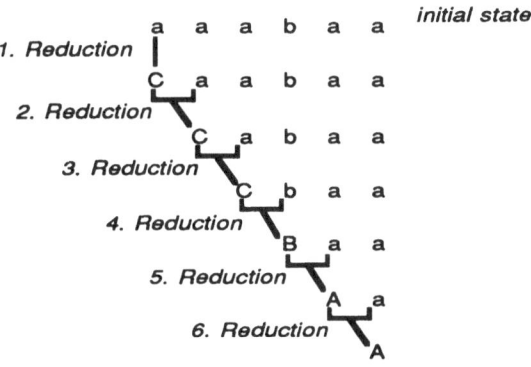

Fig. 3.2.   Analyzing a sentence of a regular grammar

We can see that for each step or state, there is just one nonterminal at the beginning of the partly reduced sentence. Each reduction depends on the current nonterminal symbol and the next input character, i.e. the next terminal symbol.

Finite Deterministic Automata

Mathematical models of devices that accept an input and produce an appropriate output are called *automata*. The characteristic of an automaton is that the input passes through various *states* to perform the output. With this in mind, the aforementioned scanning or recognition problem can be mapped onto an automaton.

The simplest automaton is a *finite deterministic automaton* (FDA). Referring to Salomaa [SALO 73] we describe an FDA heuristically as follows:

An FDA is a recognition device discriminating between input words over a fixed alphabet as illustrated in Figure 3.3.

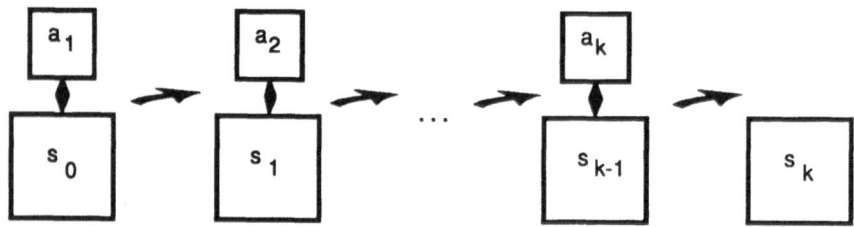

Fig. 3.3.   Finite deterministic automaton

This device consists of a storage with a *finite set of internal states* (P), among which are a specified *initial state* s_0 and a designated set F of *final states*.

Given a string $a_1a_2...a_k$ belonging to V^* (the closure of the *input vocabulary* V), the device starts at the initial state s_0 and scans the first letter a_1. The next state is uniquely determined by the actual state and the scanned letter, i.e. the device moves from state s_0 into another state s_1 (eventually $s_1 = s_0$). In state s_1, the letter a_2 is scanned. Then it moves into state s_2 and scans the next letter a_3 and so on, until it comes to the right end of the word. Note that at each step the *transition* to the next state s_{i+1} ($0 \leq i \leq k - 1$) is uniquely determined by the state s_i and the scanned letter a_{i+1}. An input word $a_1a_2...a_k$, then, uniquely determines the terminal state s_k. The input word is *accepted* by the automaton if s_k belongs to the designated set F of final states. Otherwise the word is rejected.

```
init (state, read_pos, EOT);
     (* state is start_state, read_pos is on first input
        character, end of text is set *)

WHILE  NOT EOT  DO
  readch (ch);
     (* reads one character, increments position, and
        sets EOT *)
  next_state (ch, state);
     (* changes state according to actual state and ch *)
END;

IF  state IN final_state  THEN
  accept_word
ELSE
  reject_word
END;
```

Fig. 3.4.   FDA algorithm

Such a finite automaton is said to be *deterministic* if, for each state and each input character, the automaton has just one transition state to which the automaton can change (no transitions for the empty input ε are allowed). Figure 3.4 represents the heuristic description given above as a rudimentary algorithm.

This heuristic introduction can be the basis for a more formal definition of a finite automaton. As can be seen from this introduction, a finite automaton is based on the following five essential entities:

• a finite, non-empty *set of states P*;

• the *input vocabulary V*;

• a *state transition function M*, which is a mapping from P × V into P;

• the *initial state* or *starting state* $s_0 \in P$;

• a non-empty *set of final states* $F \subset P$.

Thus, a finite automaton A can be defined more formally as a quintuple:

$$A = (P, V, M, s_0, F).$$

Other terms for finite automata are *finite-state acceptor* or just *recognizer* (since an automaton takes a string as an input and recognizes whether it belongs to a certain language or not). The state transition function M of a finite automaton A describes the relation between the states and the elements of the input vocabulary:

$$s (v) \quad \rightarrow \quad s' \, ,$$

where s, s' ∈ P, and v ∈ V. A string $\sigma \in V^*$ is accepted by A , if

$$s_0 (\sigma) \quad \rightarrow^* \quad s \, ,$$

where s ∈ F, and $\rightarrow^*$ is the reflexive transitive closure of $\rightarrow$. The language that will be accepted by a given finite automaton A (e.g. an FDA) consists of the set of all strings accepted by this finite automaton:

$$L (A) \quad = \quad \{ \sigma \in V^* \mid s_0 (\sigma) \rightarrow^* s \, , \, s \in F \} \, .$$

Then, two automata A and A' are said to be equivalent, if and only if

$$L (A) \quad = \quad L (A') \, ,$$

i.e. if they accept the same language.

Transition Diagrams and Transition Tables

It is also possible to represent an automaton graphically using a kind of transition diagram. The states of the automaton will be represented by circles which are marked with the state's name (bold circles indicate final states). The states (circles) are connected by arcs which are marked by permitted input characters. Then the arcs show the transition from one state into another state with reference to specific input values. Figure 3.5 represents a transition from state s_1 to state s_2 depending on the input a.

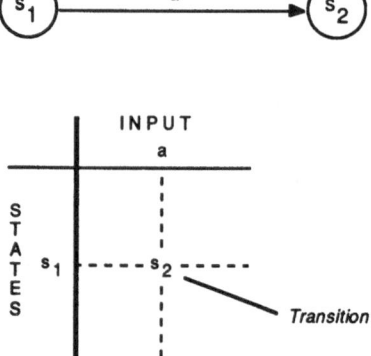

Fig. 3.5.   Transition diagram and transition table

A transition table is another representation of an automaton. The two-dimensional table contains an entry for each state and each input symbol specifying the transition (cf. Figure 3.5).

Regular Grammars and Finite Automata

It is possible to design a finite automaton A for each regular grammar G. Such an automaton A accepts the sentences of the language defined by G, i.e.

$$L(G) = L(A) .$$

A proof of this theorem can be found in [WAIT 84]. Since the tokens to be recognized in lexical analysis (i.e. identifiers, numbers, etc.) can be expressed by regular grammars, finite automata are very important for scanners and their implementation.

The correspondence between a regular grammar and a finite automaton is given by the nonterminals representing states, and the terminals forcing the transitions between states.

Figure 3.6 shows the transition diagram of a finite deterministic automaton accepting the language $L(G) = \{ a^m b a^n \mid m, n \geq 1 \}$. There are two states which have no equivalence within the set of nonterminals: the initial state I which serves just as a start-up point, and the state E which we only reach, if we analyze an incorrect sentence. Considering the recognition process illustrated in Figure 3.2, for example, we can find the fourth reduction

    Cbaa   ←   Baa

by the transition from state C to state B scanning the input symbol b (cf. Figure 3.6). All in all, we will find the following actions when analyzing the sentence *aaabaa* of Figure 3.2:

- Input a in state I: Transition to state C.

- Input a: Transition to state C.

- Input a: Transition to state C.

- Input b: Transition to state B.

- Input a: Transition to state A.

- Input a: Transition to state A.

- Finish in final state A: Accept input.

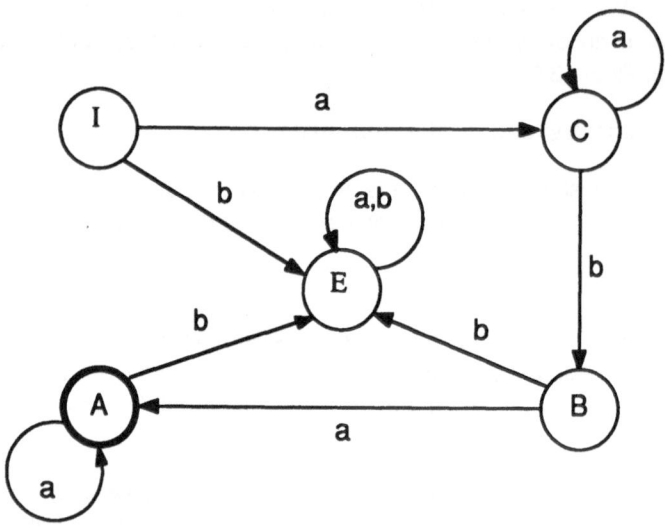

Fig. 3.6.   Finite automaton accepting $L(G) = \{ a^m b a^n \mid m, n \geq 1 \}$

Table 3.1 shows the transition table for the automaton of Figure 3.6.

Table 3.1.   Transition table according to Figure 3.6

STATES	INPUT	
	a	b
I	C	E
A	A	E
B	A	E
C	C	B
E	E	E

Now it will be easy to design the transition diagram of a finite automaton accepting, for example, Modula-2 or PASCAL identifiers which consist of letters and digits and must begin with a letter. Such identifiers might be described by the regular grammar G_2 (T_2, N_2, P_2, S_2):

$$
\begin{aligned}
T_2 &= \{ a, b, c, ..., x, y, z, 0, 1, 2, ..., 8, 9 \} \\
N_2 &= \{ ID \} \\
P_2 &= \{ ID \rightarrow \quad ID\,a \mid ID\,b \mid ... \mid ID\,z \\
&\qquad\qquad \mid ID\,0 \mid ID\,1 \mid ... \mid ID\,9 \mid a \mid b \mid ... \mid z \} \\
S_2 &= \{ ID \}
\end{aligned}
$$

The sentence *source1* is an element of the language $L(G_2)$ because it is an element of T_2^* and it can be reduced to the axiom:

source1	←	IDource1
	←	IDurce1
	←	IDrce1
	←	IDce1
	←	IDe1
	←	ID1
	←	ID

Figure 3.7 shows the transition diagram of a finite automaton accepting identifiers according to grammar G_2. The appropriate transition table is given in Table 3.2.

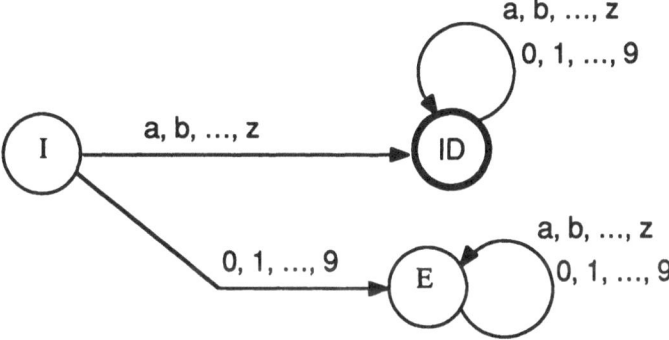

Fig. 3.7.   Finite automaton accepting identifiers

Table 3.2.   Transition table according to Figure 3.7

STATES	INPUT	
	a ... z	0 ... 9
I	ID	E
ID	ID	ID
E	E	E

Conversion into Pseudo Code

There are many ways to implement finite automata writing a program. However, since finite automata are either represented by a transition table or by a transition diagram, we will find this reflected in the implementation strategies. Therefore, programs can be designed to interpret transition tables, or they can be designed in such a way that the program's control structure corresponds directly to the states of the finite automaton.

To give an idea how to realize an automaton by reflecting the states of the automaton in the control structure of a computer program, we provide the pseudo code for the automata of Figure 3.6 and Figure 3.7 (assuming that the input symbols belong to the set of terminal symbols). We start with the finite automaton for identifiers:

```
I       readch(ch);

        if  ch in [a..z]  then

ID        while  not EOT  do  readch(ch);
          writeln("input accepted");
          halt;

        else

          while  not EOT  do  readch(ch);
E         writeln("input not accepted");
          halt;

        end;
```

Fig. 3.8.   Pseudo code for the automaton of Figure 3.7

The *halt* statement is only used for simplicity to stop the process. On the left side of this algorithm we marked the states according to Figure 3.7. For the automaton of Figure 3.6 we map each state onto a procedure as follows:

```
procedure I;
begin
  if not EOT then  readch(ch)
  else  writeln("empty input");  halt  end;
  if ch = 'a'  then  C else  E  end;
end { I };

procedure C;
begin
  while  not EOT  do
    readch(ch);
    if ch = 'b'  then  B; exit(C)  end;
  end;
  writeln("input not accepted"); halt
end { C };

procedure B;
begin
  if  not EOT  then
    readch(ch);
    if  ch = 'b'  then  E; exit(B)
    else  A; exit(B)  end;
  else
    writeln("input not accepted");  halt;
  end;
end { B };

procedure A;
begin
  while  not EOT  do
    readch(ch);
    if  ch = 'b'  then  E; exit(A)  end;
  end;
  writeln("input accepted"); halt
end { A };

procedure E;
begin
  while  not EOT  do  readch(ch)  end;
  writeln("input not accepted");  halt
end { E };

begin { Main }
  init; { Initialization of input files etc. }
  I;
end { Main }.
```

Fig. 3.9.   Pseudo code for the automaton of Figure 3.6

This pseudo code for the automaton shown in Figure 3.6 is probably not the most efficient, but it demonstrates how to map the different states of an automaton onto a computer program.

Finite Nondeterministic Automata

Finally, we want to point out once more the characteristic of a finite deterministic automaton: for each state and each input character, there exists exactly one transition state. If more than one transition state exists, we call the automaton a *finite nondeterministic automaton* (FNA); especially transitions on the empty input ε are allowed. The following example will illustrate this. Consider the automaton A_1 given by Table 3.3.

Table 3.3.   Transition table for the FNA A_1

STATES	INPUT	
	0	1
X	$\emptyset$	X, Y
Y	Y	Y

The initial state is given by X, while Y is the final state. We see that being in state X and reading an input 1 we can change to state Y or remain in state X. The automaton A_1 accepts only sentences beginning with a 1. There is no transition from X on reading a 0.

The sentence 11 will be accepted since there is a sequence of transitions to the final state Y. However, there is also a sequence of transitions, where we can remain in the initial state X which is not an element of the set of final states. This means that for a finite nondeterministic automaton, we have to check *all* possible transitions for a given sentence to be sure whether that sentence will be accepted or not. It is obvious that the checking of all possible transitions might be a very time consuming process.

Finite nondeterministic automata are not trivial to implement in a computer program. Hence, it is important to know that for any finite nondeterministic automaton A we can construct a finite deterministic automaton A' which accepts the same language as A (i.e. L (A) = L (A')). A proof of this statement can be found in [AHOU 73].

To construct an FDA from an FNA, we assume that each FDA-state corresponds to a set of FNA-states. The starting state s_0 of the FDA corresponds to a set σ_0 of FNA-states which contains the starting state of the FNA and all those states, that can be reached from this starting state having an ε input. Starting off from s_0, the next state, s_1, of the desired FDA corresponds to the set of FNA-states which can be reached by a certain input symbol (including the empty input ε) from any element of σ_0. Analogously, the FDA-state s_2 is determined for the next possible input symbol in each state of σ_0, and so on. Then, for each FDA-state which can be reached from s_0, we consider for each possible input symbol the transitions according to the corresponding sets of FNA-states, to determine new FDA-states. This process is repeated for each FDA-state until no more new states can be generated.

For example, considering the input $a_1 a_2 ... a_k$ the FDA moves from the initial state to a state representing a subset of the states of the FNA that are reachable from the FNA's initial state along some path labeled $a_1 a_2 ... a_k$. The construction process introduced above is often referred to as *subset construction*. For more details see [AHOS 86].

Thus, considering our automaton A_1 we can say that the state Y of a deterministic automaton represents the subset { X, Y } of states of the FNA A_1. Additionally, we can introduce a new state Z which corresponds to the empty set of states in A_1. Then, the deterministic equivalence to A_1 is given in Table 3.4.

Table 3.4.   Transition table for FDA A_2 accepting the same language as A_1

STATES	INPUT	
	0	1
X	Z	Y
Y	Y	Y
Z	Z	Z

In this book we will only deal with finite deterministic automata. However, considering bottom-up syntax analysis, we will find an example for a finite nondeterministic automata for which, then, a FDA will be constructed (cf. Chapter 4). This construction will be an example of the subset construction introduced above.

3.2   The Scanner

The interaction between the scanner (lexical analysis) and the parser (syntax analysis) is shown in Figure 3.10 (here the scanner is assumed to be a server for the parser). The scanner reads input characters (the source code) and produces sequences of symbols and symbol values which are analyzed syntactically by the parser. Thus, the scanning or recognition process can be understood as a transformation of a character stream into a "reduced" symbol stream. Here, the term "reduced" means that the input is filtered to get rid of those elements of the program text which are just used to make the program readable for the programmer (this is comparable to the application of reduction mechanisms in natural language document processing in terms of information retrieval).

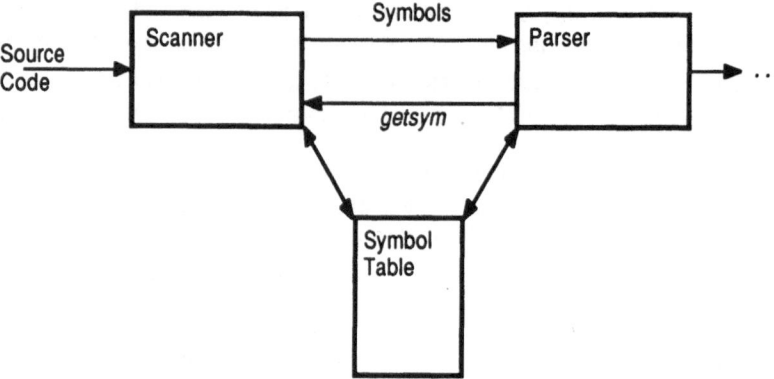

Fig. 3.10. Interaction between scanner and parser

Skipping Separators

Spaces, tabulators, comments and new lines are called separators. They can be very numerous in a source code, as it is exemplified in Figure 3.11.

```
CONST|    MaxLnl...=..100;.(* length of lines *)↵
   |      Maxch....=..20;..(* length of names *)↵
   |      NoOfRw...=..11;..(* number of reserved words *)↵
   |      Blank....=..'.';↵
```

Fig. 3.11. Separators in a source code

Skipping separators is in general a trivial task except skipping nested comments which is a recursive process. This is shown in Figure 3.12. To simplify matters, we assume that a comment starts and ends with a single character; these comment delimiters are kept in the variables SC (start) and EC (end), respectively.

```
PROCEDURE Skip_Com;
BEGIN

  readch (ch);
  WHILE  (ch <> EC) AND NOT EOF  DO
    IF  ch = SC  THEN  Skip_Com;  readch (ch)
    ELSE  readch (ch)  END;
  END;
  IF  EOF  THEN  Error (...)  END;

END Skip_Com;
```

Fig. 3.12. Skipping comments

Recognizing Operators and Names

Symbols like

> +   –   *   /

are easy to recognize because each of these symbols consists of a single character which does not occur at the beginning of any other symbol. However, symbols like

> <   <=   and   >   >=

begin with the same character. In such situations the scanner has to *look ahead one character* to determine the symbol correctly. Here we have to notice that we have probably already read the first character of the next symbol. This happens also when scanning a numeral or an identifier or a word symbol.

The recognition of identifiers and keywords (or reserved words) in a character stream is a trivial task; it is based on finite automata as described in the previous section. The non-trivial task the scanner has to fulfil here is to distinguish between identifiers and keywords. This can be done using symbol tables or an additional data structure containing all reserved words. Symbol tables are described in more detail in the following section.

Numbers

A numeral has to be transformed by the scanner into the numeral symbol and the value of the numeral. This can be done using the algorithm shown in Figure 3.13 for integers.

```
num   := 0;   symbol := numeral;

WHILE   ch IN Digits  DO
  digit := ORD(ch) - ORD('0');
  IF  num <= (MaxInt - digit) DIV 10   THEN
    num := num * 10  +  digit;
    readch (ch);
  ELSE
    num := 0;
    Error (…)   (* skip the remaining digits *)
  END;
END;
```

Fig. 3.13. Recognition of numerals

The algorithm in Figure 3.13 contains the constant MaxInt which represents the largest possible integer on a certain computer. It is used to avoid overflows.

3.3 Symbol Tables

A symbol table is an *information structure* for managing the names (identifiers and reserved words) of the source code. It supports semantic or context-sensitive checking as well as the code generation process. The information stored in the table will be completed during the analyzing phases and will then be used for code generation. In general, a symbol table consists of names and attributes as shown in Figure 3.14.

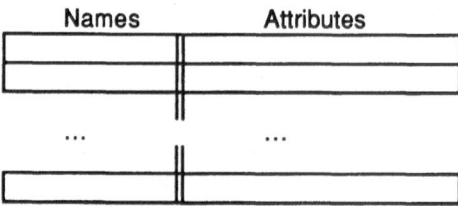

Fig 3.14. A simplified symbol table

The information stored in a symbol table will vary from compiler to compiler and from language to language, i.e. it depends on the language as well as on the designer of a compiler, which information will be included in a symbol table. In this section we therefore want to put the emphasis on the organization and data structures of a symbol table rather than on its contents. Anyhow, a few general remarks on a symbol table's contents can be made. Clearly, the *Names*-field contains the (identifier) names while the attributes can be among others:

- a names type and/or value;

- the dimension or number of parameters for a procedure;

- a pointer to where a name is declared and referenced;

- some kind of address, usually an offset;

- some scope information in case of a block-oriented language.

If a name in a symbol table refers to a constant, we need to store not only the constant's type, but also the value of the constant. Pointers to where a name is declared and referenced can support the generation of error listings, while scope information obviously will be needed for all block-oriented languages allowing the declaration of the same name in different blocks.

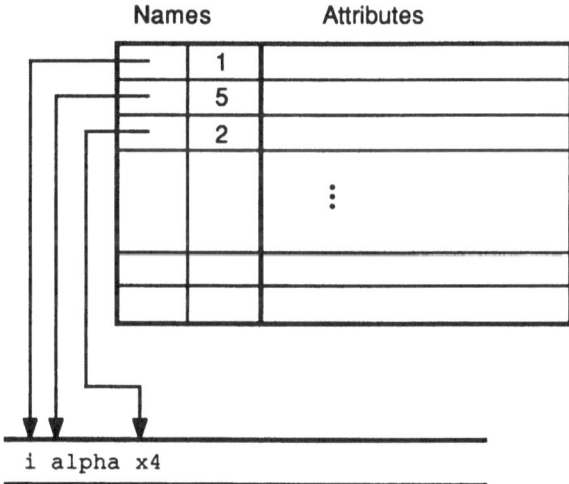

Fig. 3.15. Storing names using pointers and length of names

There are many ways of handling variable length names. If the considered programming language allows only names up to a maximum number of characters, e.g. six characters, the handling of the names is easy, i.e. the names can be stored in a fixed-sized maximum-length name-field. But if the names can be of an arbitrary length or if the maximum length of a name is relatively large, e.g. 32 characters, this direct storage method is not applicable or might be very storage inefficient. A popular approach to handling such names in a symbol table is splitting the name-field of the table into two subfields, one containing a pointer to a separate string table and the other containing the length of the name. The pointer specifies the position of the first character of the name in the string table. This is shown in Figure 3.15.

Considering the above-mentioned functionality of a symbol table (i.e. storage of names and appropriate information), we will find that we need just two operations on it:

- insert, and

- lookup.

We can search for an identifier (or a name in general) using the lookup-function. If the search was not successful, a new identifier can be inserted using the insert function. Obviously, we can distinguish between identifiers and reserved words, if the symbol table is initialized with the reserved words.

The lookup operation must be implemented using a sophisticated algorithm and/or data structure because programs of some thousand lines of source code may contain some hundred different identifiers. Investigations (not necessarily representative) considering different software projects with approximately 5000 to 10000 lines of Modula-2 source code have shown that the programmers used about 500 to 1500 different names. Since these names do not only occur once but many times searching for a name can become very time consuming if done in the wrong way. Brinch Hansen reports in his book some investigations on the number of comparisons using different search methods [BRIN 85].

The most inefficient search is *linear searching* using a linear list as the data structure of the symbol table, i.e. having the table organized as a linked list of records containing the name and attribute fields (see Figure 3.16, where n1, n2, etc. represent the names).

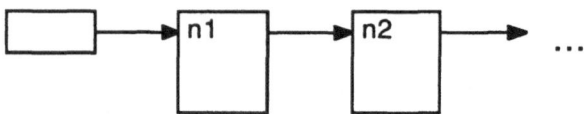

Fig. 3.16. Linked list

A linked list is the simplest way to organize a symbol table, but the search on such a list is purely sequential. If the list is not ordered, we might have to check the entire table before knowing whether a name is or is not included in the table. On average, we will find a name by comparing n/2 names, where n is the total number of names in the table. Thus, the cost of search is proportional to n.

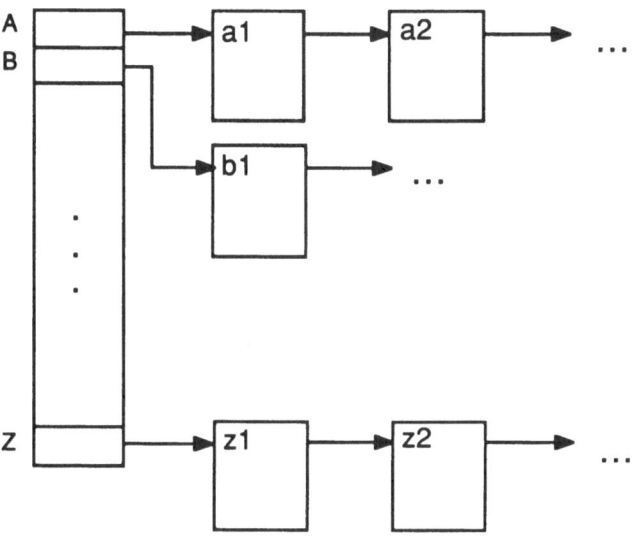

Fig. 3.17. Symbol table for letter indexing

Linear searching can be improved using so-called *letter indexing* or even *bigram indexing*. Instead of a single linked list we have an array of linked record lists. For letter indexing we use a one-dimensional array [A..Z] of linked lists as shown in Figure 3.17, assuming that names can only begin with upper case letters (to simplify matters). In Figure 3.17 the elements a1, a2, b1, etc. represent the first, second, etc. names beginning with A, B, ..., Z.

For bigram indexing we need a two-dimensional array [A..Z, A..Z0..9¢] of records (¢ stands for space). Bigram indexing is shown in Figure 3.18. Here we use the first or first and second character of a name to select the list which then will be searched linearly (again za1, za2, ... represent the first, second, ... names beginning with ZA). For one-character names, the second character is assumed to be ¢.

When analyzing a program text, we will probably find that many array indices have a reference to a nil pointer, because there are no identifiers beginning with the particular character(s). Thus, the cost of search is less than n/2 using letter indexing but only in those cases where the first characters of names are uniformly distributed. Similar statements are valid for bigram indexing. However, from statistical investigations of natural languages we know that letters (and especially the first ones of a word) are not uniformly distributed (e.g. see [SUEN 79]). This can also be assumed for the names of a program, even for those names which sound sometimes rather artificial. In addition, everyone of us knows from his own experience that programmers tend to structure or to cluster variable names, e.g. *bank*, *bankintr1*, *bankintr2*, etc. This means that using letter or bigram indexing, some names might be found very quickly and others very slowly.

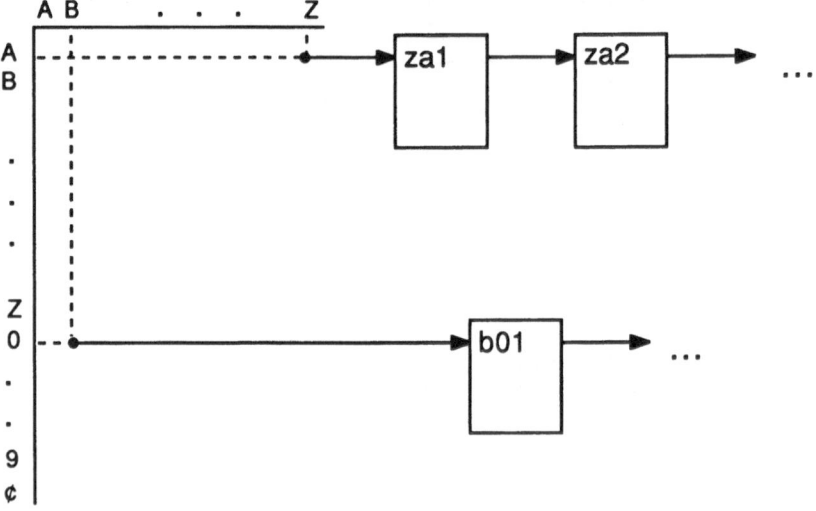

Fig. 3.18. Symbol table for bigram indexing

The most important disadvantage here are the very varying access times. So, what we need are algorithms performing a more unique distribution of these access times. A first improvement could be obtained for bigram indexing when using the first and last (instead of the first and second) character to determine the entry to the table. This is a very simple method which, moreover, allows an easy calculation of a name's index address. Bigram indexing using the first and last character of a name performs suitable results in cases of clustered names.

Another popular alternative to the above-mentioned methods is *hashing*. Using hash symbol tables, the cost of search is essentially independent of n, the number of names in the table, i.e. the search time is constant for any n. Hashing or *hash-coding* means that the address of a name's location is a function of the name itself, and it is determined by some mapping algorithm applied to the name. When searching, the same algorithm is applied to the search key. Thus, hashing denotes that names are not stored in some (alphabetical) order, on the contrary, the order looks chaotic (as implied by the term *hash*), but the chaos is well-defined.

The following has to be noticed:

- The *size N* of the address space must be determined, i.e. we must decide how many names we are expecting. Let H (v) be the address of a name v. Then,

$$H (v) \in [1, N] .$$

- A *function* f (v) to transform the alphanumerical names v into an integer must be found. For example, let $v = c_1 c_2 \dots c_k$ be a name of length k. Then, f (v) could be defined as

$$f (v) = ord (c_1) + ord (c_k) + 16 * k ,$$

where ord is the ordinal position function (cf. [MCKE 74] or [CICH 80]). This is just one example from a long list of transformation functions which are published.

- A *mapping* from the integer representation of a name v into the address space [1, N] must be found. The most common mapping is given by

$$H (v) = f (v) \; MOD \; N + 1 \quad \Rightarrow \quad H (v) \in [1, N] .$$

- The size of the address space *N should be a prime* to guarantee a uniform distribution of the calculated addresses [MAUR 68].

The introduced transformation function f (v) bears some resemblance to the improved bigram indexing method, since in both cases the first and the last character of the name v is involved. Based on these functions, the ASCII-character set, and an address space N = 13, we can consider the following examples:

$$
\begin{aligned}
H \, (ALPHA1) \quad &= \quad f \, (ALPHA1) \; MOD \; 13 + 1 \\
&= \quad (\, ord \, (A) + ord \, (1) + 16 * 6 \,) \; MOD \; 13 + 1 \\
&= \quad (\, 65 + 49 + 96 \,) \; MOD \; 13 + 1 \\
&= \quad 210 \; MOD \; 13 + 1 \\
&= \quad 3
\end{aligned}
$$

$$
\begin{aligned}
H \, (a) \quad &= \quad f \, (a) \; MOD \; 13 + 1 \\
&= \quad (\, ord \, (a) + ord \, (a) + 16 * 1 \,) \; MOD \; 13 + 1 \\
&= \quad (\, 97 + 97 + 16 \,) \; MOD \; 13 + 1 \\
&= \quad 210 \; MOD \; 13 + 1 \\
&= \quad 3
\end{aligned}
$$

These examples show us the problems that can happen with hash coding: Two different names are coded to the same index (address). Now we understand why it is important that the hash-function distributes the names (i.e. their addresses) uniformly among the address space. But even the 'best' hash functions do not guarantee that all calculated addresses are distinctive. Therefore, we need some strategies to handle such *collisions*; the most popular strategies to generate secondary indexes are:

- *Direct chaining*: All names v with an identical primary index H (v) are linked together to an ordinary linked list. This solution is very similar to letter or bigram indexing.

- *Open addressing*: When a collision occurs, the name is inserted into the next available space in the table. When retrieving from the hash table, a linear search (after not finding the name at the hashed location) is conducted, starting at the hashed location, until the string is found.

More about hashing can be found in [MORR 68], [BRIN 85], [TREM 85], or [AHOS 87], while tree structured symbol tables (i.e. binary tree organization, balanced trees, AVL, B-trees etc.) are dealt with in [TREM 85] or in a general manner in [WIRT 76].

3.4   Lexical Analysis of PL/0

To design a PL/0-scanner we use a finite automaton as defined in section 3.1. Figure 3.19 represents a rudimentary transition diagram of the automaton that recognizes symbols of the language PL/0.

The scanner must be able to recognize the following symbols:

- reserved words,

- names of identifiers,

- numerals,

- operators.

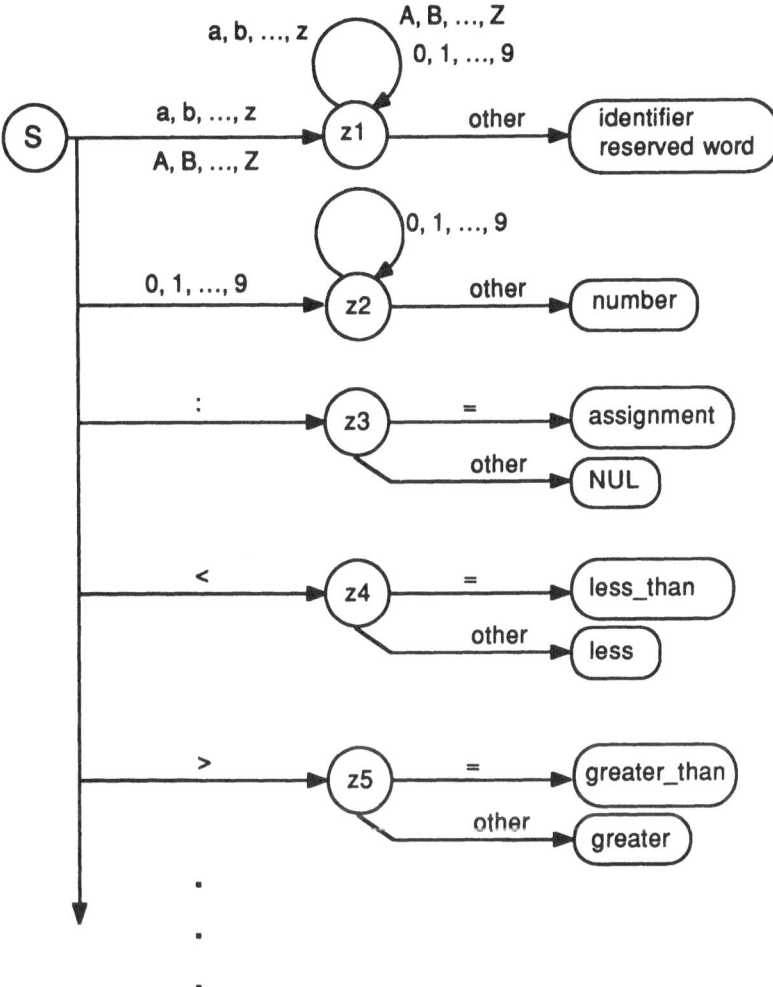

Fig. 3.19. Rudimentary transition diagram for a PL/0-scanner

To conclude this chapter we give the code for a PL/0 scanner. We assume that the scanner is a subroutine of the parser, i.e. the scanner consists of a procedure Get_Symbol which provides the next symbol to the parser using the global variable symbol.

```
CONST
    MaxLnl   =  100;  (* length of lines *)
    Maxch    =  20;   (* length of names *)
    NoOfRw   =  11;   (* number of reserved words *)
    Blank    =  ' ';

TYPE
    symbols = (nul, ident, number, plus, minus, times,
               slash, oddsym, eql, neq, lss, leq, gtr,
               geq, lparen, rparen, comma, semicolon,
               period, becomes, beginsym, endsym, ifsym,
               thensym, whilesym, dosym, callsym,
               constsym, varsym, procsym);

VAR
    linepos   : INTEGER;
    linelngth : INTEGER;
    num       : INTEGER;
    line      : ARRAY [1..MaxLnl] OF CHAR;
    source    : FILE OF CHAR;
    ch        : CHAR;
    id        : PACKED ARRAY [1..Maxch] OF CHAR;
    rword     : PACKED ARRAY [1..NoOfRw] OF CHAR;
                    (* initialized with reserved words *)
    wsym      : PACKED ARRAY [1..NoOfRw] OF symbols;
                    (* initialized with the representation
                       of reserved words *)
    ssym      : PACKED ARRAY [CHAR] OF symbols;
                    (* initialized with the representation
                       of special symbols *)
    symbol    : symbols;

PROCEDURE Get_Symbol;
VAR   i, j, k   : INTEGER;
      digit     : INTEGER;

  PROCEDURE GetChar;
  BEGIN
    IF  linepos = linelngth  THEN
      IF  EOF(source)  THEN  Error(...)  END;
      linelngth = 0;
      linepos = 0;
      WHILE  NOT EOLN(source)  DO
        INC(linelngth);
        IF  linelngth > MaxLnl  THEN  Error(...)  END;
        READ (source, line(linelngth));
      END;
```

```
    IF  NOT EOF(source)  THEN  READLN (source)  END;
    INC(linelngth);
    line(linelngth) := 0C;
  END;
  INC(linepos);
  ch := line(linepos);
END (* GetChar *);

BEGIN (* Get_Symbol *)
  WHILE  ch = Blank  DO  GetChar  END;
  IF  (Upper(ch) IN ['A'..'Z']  THEN
    (* identifier or reserved word *)
    FOR  k := 1  TO  Maxch  DO  id[k] := Blank  END;
    k := 0;
    REPEAT
      IF  k < Maxch  THEN
        INC(k);
        id[k] := ch;
      END;
      GetChar;
    UNTIL  NOT  (ch IN ['a'..'z','A'..'Z','0'..'9']);
    i := 1;
    j := NoOfRw;
    REPEAT
      k := (i + j) DIV 2;
      IF  id <= rword[k]  THEN  j := k - 1  END;
      IF  id >= rword[k]  THEN  i := k + 1  END;
    UNTIL  (i > j);
    IF  (i - 1 > j)  THEN  symbol := wsym[k]
                     ELSE  symbol := ident  END;
  ELSIF  (ch IN Digits)  THEN
    num  := 0;
    symbol := number;
    WHILE  ch IN Digits  DO
      digit := ORD(ch) - ORD('0');
      IF  num <= (MaxInt - digit) DIV 10  THEN
        num := num * 10  + digit;
        GetChar
      ELSE
        num := 0;
        Error (...)
        (* skip the remaining digits *)
      END
    END
  ELSIF  ch = ':'  THEN
    GetChar;
    IF  ch = '='  THEN
      symbol := becomes;
```

```
      GetChar
    ELSE
      symbol := nul
    END;
  ELSIF  ch = '<'  THEN
    GetChar;
    IF  ch = '='  THEN
      symbol := le;
      GetChar
    ELSE
      symbol := less
    END;
  ELSIF  ch = '>'  THEN
    GetChar;
    IF  ch = '='  THEN
      symbol := ge;
      GetChar
    ELSE
      symbol := greater
    END;
  ELSE
      symbol := ssym[ch];
      GetChar
  END;
END (* Get_Symbol *);
```

4 Syntax Analysis and Parser Construction

In Chapter 3 we gave an introduction to the lexical analysis, i.e. we showed how the scanner recognizes the symbols within the character stream of the source code. These symbol sequences are sequentially analyzed by the *parser*. Thus, the parser decides whether a certain sequence of symbols will be accepted by the considered programming language.

As shown in Chapter 2 there are two main methods of doing the syntactical analysis: *top-down parsing* and *bottom-up parsing*. The most efficient top-down and bottom-up parsers are based on so-called *LL-* and *LR-grammars*, respectively. These grammars are context-free. Thus, before starting to explain these two parsing methods, we have a more detailed look at those grammars.

4.1 Top-down Analysis

Top-down analysis is based on LL-grammars which allow a dead lock free analysis of an input sentence.

4.1.1 LL-grammars

In Chapter 2 we learned that it is possible to make a wrong decision when constructing a parse tree, because there were different alternatives in a certain situation (i.e. informally spoken that the grammar was not exact enough). Therefore, we postulate the following rule for parsers:

> *For each production of the form*
> $$A \quad \rightarrow \quad \sigma_1 \mid \sigma_2 \mid ... \mid \sigma_n$$
> *we should always be able to choose the correct alternative for the generation of a parse tree.*

To fulfil this rule we need some additional information, i.e. we need to know

1) the set of all terminal symbols that may occur at the beginning of a sentence that can be derived from an arbitrary sequence of symbols;

2) the set of all terminal symbols that may follow after a nonterminal.

These are the so-called *FIRST* and *FOLLOW* sets.

Let G (N, T, P, S) be a grammar and α be an arbitrary sequence of symbols, i.e. $\alpha \in (N \cup T)^*$. Then we define the set of terminals that can be the beginnings of any derivable sentence as

$$\text{FIRST}(\alpha) \quad = \quad \{ t \mid t \in T_\varepsilon \wedge \alpha \rightarrow^* t\alpha' \},$$

where $T_\varepsilon = T \cup \{ \varepsilon \}$.

Let X be a nonterminal symbol. Then, FOLLOW(X) is the set of all terminal symbols that can occur immediately to the right of X:

$$\text{FOLLOW}(X) \quad = \quad \{ t \mid t \in T \wedge S \rightarrow^* \alpha X t \beta \}.$$

The algorithms to construct the FIRST and FOLLOW sets are shown in Figure 4.1 and Figure 4.2, respectively. The function INCLUDE (a, B) means that a becomes an element of set B.

```
FOR  ( ∀ X ∈ T )  DO  INCLUDE (X, FIRST(X))  END;

FOR  ( ∀ X ∈ N )  DO
  FOR  ( ∀ (X → Σ) ∈ P )  DO
    IF  (Σ = ε)  THEN
        INCLUDE (ε, FIRST(X))
    ELSE   (* Σ = σ1 σ2 … σk *)
        i := 1;
        WHILE  (i < k) AND (σi →* ε)  DO  INC(i)  END;
        INCLUDE (FIRST(σi), FIRST(X));
    END;
  END;
END;
```

Fig. 4.1.   Algorithm to construct FIRST-sets

```
FOR  ( ∀ X ∈ N )  DO
  FOLLOW(X) := ∅
  FOR  ( ∀ (Y → αXβ) ∈ P )   DO
    IF  (β = ε) OR (β →* ε)  THEN
      INCLUDE (FOLLOW(Y), FOLLOW(X));   (* 1 *)
    IF  (β ≠ ε)  THEN
      INCLUDE (FIRST(β)∩T, FOLLOW(X));
    END;
  END;
END;
```

Fig. 4.2.   Algorithm to construct FOLLOW-sets

The line in the algorithm of Figure 4.2 which is marked by the comment (* 1 *) represents a situation in the production set like

$$W \rightarrow YZ$$
$$V \rightarrow WX$$

where X is an element of FOLLOW(Z) or, more general, any element of FOLLOW(W) is in the set FOLLOW(Z).

We call a context-free grammar G (N, T, P, S) an *LL(1)-grammar*, if it has the following characteristics:

C1)   For each production

$$A \rightarrow \sigma_1 | \sigma_2 | ... | \sigma_n$$

it is required that

$$FIRST(\sigma_i) \cap FIRST(\sigma_j) = \emptyset \quad \forall i \neq j.$$

C2) If the empty string ε can be derived from a nonterminal X, then it is required that

$$FIRST(X) \cap FOLLOW(X) = \emptyset.$$

The first "L" of LL(1) means that the input will be read from left to right, while the second "L" indicates leftmost derivations. The "1" means that we look ahead one symbol at any step of the parse process.

The characteristic C1 means that for a given input string there exists just one possible production at a certain state of the derivation, i.e. it will be obvious which alternative of a production should be applied. For example, considering the following grammar G (cf. [WIRT 86]):

T = { x, y, z }
N = { A, B, C }
P = { A → B | C
        B → x B | y
        C → x C | z }
S = { A } .

The sentence *xxz* is an element of L(G). A leftmost derivation of the sentence (to generate a top-down parse tree) can probably start with the following derivations

A   → B
           → x B
           → x x B

At this point it can be recognized that z cannot be derived from B. This dead lock occurred because

FIRST(B) ∩ FIRST(C) = { x } ≠ ∅ .

When starting from the axiom of the grammar and just looking one character ahead it is not decidable whether A should be replaced by B or by C because both alternatives can produce the starting x's of the input string. (Note: A look ahead of two symbols is no solution for the given problem because it will not work for any sentence containing more than two x's at the beginning). The grammar

T = { x, y, z }
N = { A, B }
P = { A → B | x A
        B → y | z }
S = { A }

generates the same language as the grammar given above and fulfils characteristic C1. Thus, there is no problem to derive the sentence *xxz* from the axiom of that grammar:

A   → x A
           → x x A
           → x x B
           → x x z

Characteristic C2 helps to avoid dead locks occurring in (BNF-) productions of the form

$$A \quad \rightarrow \quad \{x\} \quad \text{or} \quad A \quad \rightarrow \quad [x]$$

where arbitrary occurrences (including 0 times) are allowed. Let us consider the following grammar (cf. [WIRT 86]):

$$
\begin{aligned}
T &= \{x\} \\
N &= \{A, B\} \\
P &= \{A \quad \rightarrow \quad B x \\
&\phantom{=\{} B \quad \rightarrow \quad x \mid \varepsilon \} \\
S &= \{A\}.
\end{aligned}
$$

When trying to recognize the sentence x, it is possible to get into a dead lock when starting with the following derivations:

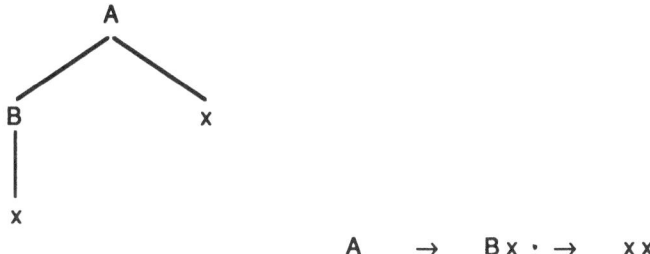

$$A \quad \rightarrow \quad B x \cdot \rightarrow \quad x x$$

Here we should have chosen the production $B \rightarrow \varepsilon$ instead of $B \rightarrow x$. But a definite decision is only be possible, if it is clear whether the x will be generated as a follow symbol or as a first symbol of B. This requires that the intersection of FIRST(B) and FOLLOW(B) is the empty set.

FIRST and FOLLOW sets are simple to understand, when considering some examples; therefore, we define grammar G_3 (T_3, N_3, P_3, S_3):

$$
\begin{aligned}
T_3 &= \{+, a, b, c\} \\
N_3 &= \{S, A, B\} \\
P_3 &= \{S \quad \rightarrow \quad A \mid B \\
&\phantom{=\{} A \quad \rightarrow \quad cA{+}b \mid a \\
&\phantom{=\{} B \quad \rightarrow \quad cB{+}a \mid b \} \\
S_3 &= \{S\}
\end{aligned}
$$

This grammar accepts the language L_3

$$L_3 (G_3) \quad = \quad \{c^n a(+b)^n \mid n \geq 0\} \cup \{c^n b(+a)^n \mid n \geq 0\}$$

where c^n, $(+b)^n$, and $(+a)^n$ means that these elements occur n times. The FIRST and FOLLOW sets of the grammar G_3 are shown in Table 4.1.

Table 4.1.   FIRST and FOLLOW sets of G_3

σ	FIRST (σ)	FOLLOW (σ)
a	a	undefined
b	b	undefined
c	c	undefined
+	+	undefined
A	c, a	+
B	c, b	+
S	a, b, c	∅

Grammar G_3 (T_3, N_3, P_3, S_3) is not an LL(1)-grammar, because it does not fulfil characteristic C1:

FIRST (A) ∩ FIRST (B) = { c } ≠ ∅ .

This intersection should be the empty set, because of the production S → A | B.

As a second example we want to consider a grammar which allows the generation of sentences like

```
program
        declaration;
        declaration;
begin
        statement;
        statement;
        statement
end.
```

(the formatting information is not specified by the grammar, of course). The grammar G_4 is given by the sets

T_4 =   { b, d, e, p, s, ;, . }
N_4 =   { A, X, Y }
P_4 =   { A   →   p X
                X   →   d ; X | b s Y e .
                Y   →   ε | ; s Y }
S_4 =   { A }

where the following abbreviations are used: b = begin, d = declaration, e = end, p = program, s = statement. Grammar G_4 is an LL(1)-grammar because it fulfils characteristic C1

$$\text{FIRST (d ; X)} \cap \text{FIRST (b s Y e .)} = \{d\} \cap \{b\} = \varnothing$$

$$\text{FIRST (}\varepsilon\text{)} \cap \text{FIRST (; s Y)} = \{\varepsilon\} \cap \{;\} = \varnothing$$

as well as characteristic C2

$$\text{FIRST (Y)} \cap \text{FOLLOW (Y)} = \{\varepsilon, ;\} \cap \{e\} = \varnothing .$$

From the definition of an LL(1)-grammar it follows that such a grammar is *unambiguous* and that it *can never be left-recursive*. This is obvious, because a grammar G is said to be ambiguous, if there is a word in L (G) possessing two leftmost derivations (from the initial letter). That means, there must be a production with two alternatives producing the same first-symbols and, therefore, the intersection of the corresponding FIRST-sets are not empty. For example, we can consider the grammar which is given by the following production set and which generates the same language as grammar G_0:

$$P \quad = \quad \{E \quad \rightarrow \quad E\,O\,E \mid (E) \mid x \mid y$$
$$O \quad \rightarrow \quad + \mid - \mid {}^* \mid / \}$$

This is an ambiguous grammar as it was shown in Chapter 2 and the intersection of the appropriate FIRST-sets is not empty:

$$\text{FIRST (E O E)} \cap \text{FIRST ((E))} = \{(, x, y\} \cap \{(\} \neq \varnothing .$$

To prove that a LL-grammar cannot be left recursive, we assume such a grammar has a left-recursive production $X \rightarrow X\sigma_1$ and that X can be derived to the empty string ($X \rightarrow^* \varepsilon$). It follows that

$$\text{FIRST (}\sigma_1\text{)} \subset \text{FIRST (X)}$$

and

$$\text{FIRST (}\sigma_1\text{)} \subset \text{FOLLOW (X)}$$

which is a contradiction to C2. On the other hand, if X cannot be derived to ε a production

$$X \rightarrow \sigma_2 \quad \text{and} \quad \sigma_2 \rightarrow^* t , \quad \text{where t is an element of T}$$

must exist. Then, it follows that

$$\text{FIRST}(X\sigma_1) \cap \text{FIRST}(\sigma_2) = \{t\}$$

which is a contradiction to C1.

For example, we consider the following simple left-recursive grammar G which generates the language $L(G) = \{ba^n \mid n \geq 0\}$:

T	=	$\{a, b\}$
N	=	$\{A\}$
P	=	$\{A \rightarrow Aa \mid b\}$
S	=	$\{A\}$

where FIRST(Aa) = FIRST(b) = { b } and therefore characteristic C1 for an LL(1)-grammar is not fulfilled.

LL(1)-grammars are preferably used for top-down parsing. They allow an analysis with no dead locks.

Now that we have introduced LL-grammars, we want to start with general *top-down parsing* which is often referred to as *recursive descent parsing* (or *predictive parsing*). The general principles of recursive descent parsers are shown in the following section while top-down parsing using parse tables is shown in section 4.1.3.

4.1.2   Recursive Descent Strategy

The basic concepts of top-down parsing were introduced in Chapter 2. Top-down analysis can be thought of as an attempt to find a leftmost derivation for a given input and by doing so to generate a parse tree from the top (i.e. the axiom of the grammar) down to the leaves of the tree. Thus, when analyzing an input, a top-down parser starts with the grammar's axiom. Then, as long as there are nonterminal leaves, one of the productions belonging to these leaves will be selected to generate the children of the nonterminal leaf, according to the right side of the selected production. An input is correct, if the sequence of the generated terminal leaves matches the sequence of input symbols.

This general method of recursive descent parsing can also be applied to grammars other then LL(1)-grammars, but only LL(1)-grammars will guarantee that no dead locks and, therefore, no backtracking will occur. Thus, a production selected for a nonterminal leaf is always valid. We define grammar G_5 (T_5, N_5, P_5, S_5) to demonstrate this problem :

T_5	=	$\{a, b, c, d, e\}$
N_5	=	$\{S, A, B\}$

$$P_5 \;=\; \{S \;\rightarrow\; cAd \mid dBc$$
$$A \;\rightarrow\; ab \mid a$$
$$B \;\rightarrow\; ae \mid A \}$$
$$S_5 \;=\; \{S\}$$

Grammar G_5 is not LL(1), because

$$FIRST(ab) \cap FIRST(a) \;=\; FIRST(ae) \cap FIRST(A) \;=\; \{a\} \;\neq\; \varnothing.$$

We suppose the input to be *dac*. To get a top-down parse tree for this input we first have to generate the root of the tree, i.e. we need a tree with just one node which is marked S. The pointer on the input string is on *d*. Using the first production for S we can expand the tree as follows:

Then, the leftmost leaf is labeled c and does not match the first symbol of the input string. Thus, we will choose the alternative production expanding the tree as follows:

Now, the leftmost leaf, labeled d, matches the first symbol of the input string. Therefore, we can move the pointer to the second symbol of the input string (*a*) and we can consider the next leaf which is labeled B. In the next step, B is expanded using the first alternative:

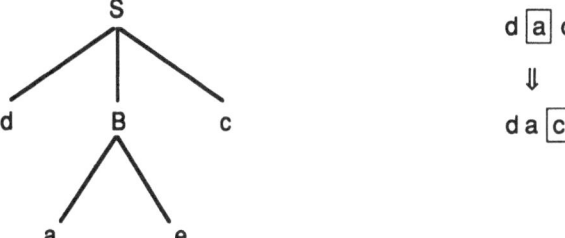

The leftmost leaf of the subtree starting at B, labeled a, matches the second symbol of the input string, so we can advance the pointer to *c*, the third symbol of the input string. We compare the next leaf to *c*. Since *c* does not match *e*, we report a failure and go back to B hoping to find another alternative.

By doing so, we have to reset the pointer on the input string for one position, i.e. we have to set it on position 2. Now, we expand B to A and afterwards expand A using the first alternative:

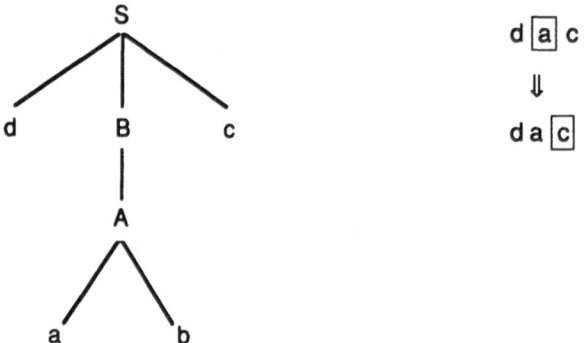

Again we have a match for the second input symbol, so we can advance the pointer once again to *c*. Comparing c with the next leaf we will find one more failure. Thus, we have to go back one step, i.e. we have to go back to A to see whether there is another alternative. Of course, we also have to reset the pointer on the input string to *a*. Trying the second alternative for A we will get the following tree:

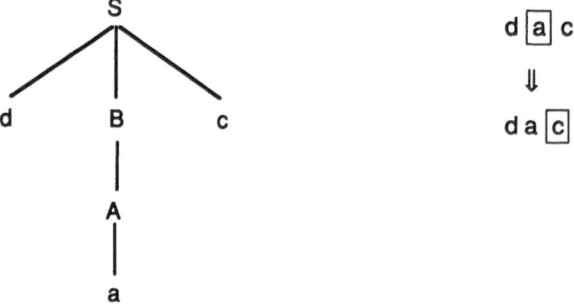

The second input symbol matches the leaf *a*, and the third input symbol matches the leaf labeled *c*. Thus, we have produced a parse tree for the string *dac* and we can stop and report success.

We have seen that top-down analysis will probably require backtracking, i.e. the repeated reading of the same input, when analyzing a sentence generated by a grammar which is not LL(1). This occurs because the intersection of the FIRST-sets of different alternatives of a production are not empty. Backtracking is not impossible to implement, but it can be a risky operation in the analyzing process when using a left recursive grammar (because of the possibility of infinite loops). Such properties of a grammar prevent the writing of a recursive descent parser from being straightforward.

Now, let us consider the top-down generation of the parse tree for a sentence generated by an LL(1)-grammar, having a look ahead facility of 1 symbol. Applying the concepts of recursive descent parsing to grammar G_4 (which is LL(1)) and assuming the input to be

  program begin statement end .   ($\equiv$ p b s e .) ,

we find the generation of the parse tree starting once more by using the axiom as the root. The pointer on the input string is on *p*. The children of the root are determined by the axiom's production:

The leftmost leaf labeled *p* matches the first input symbol, so that the pointer on the input string can be moved to *b* and the children of the next nonterminal leaf (X) are determined by that production $X \rightarrow \sigma_i$, where $b \in FIRST(\sigma_i)$. Thus, the tree will be expanded to:

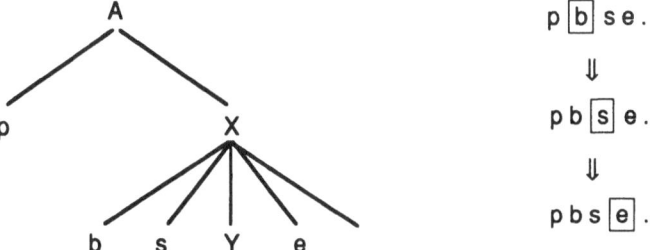

Obviously, the left child of X must match the current input symbol. This is why the pointer on the input string is advanced to *s*, which is matched by the next terminal leaf. Thus, the input pointer is advanced to *e*. The next leaf represents the nonterminal Y and, since *e* ∉ FIRST(;sY), Y will be reduced to the empty string:

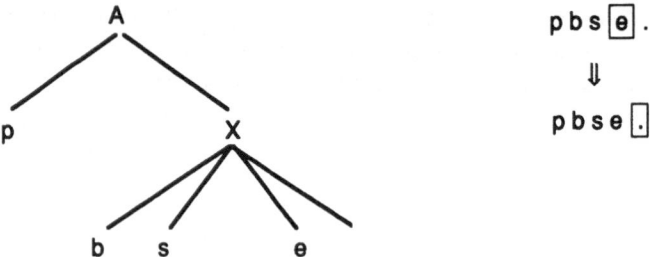

The matching of the rest of the input sequence is obvious.

Structure of a recursive descent parser

The most popular way to implement a recursive descent parser is to associate a procedure with each nonterminal of the grammar. Assume G (T, N, P, S) to be an LL(1)-grammar, where N = {N_0, N_1, N_2, ..., N_m}, S = N_0. The nonterminals correspond to the syntactical categories that should be recognized. Therefore, they will be mapped to (recursive) procedures. When using an LL(1)-grammar the look ahead symbol determines exactly the procedure called for each nonterminal and, thus, requires no backtracking. The parse tree is implicitly given by the sequence of procedure calls, as shown later on.

These procedures are embedded into a main program containing also an error-procedure and a procedure which provides the next symbol (`Get_Symbol`, as known from Chapter 3). The principal structure of a recursive descent parser for the above-mentioned grammar G is shown in Figure 4.2.

```
PROGRAM Parser;

   PROCEDURE Error (…);
   PROCEDURE N0; . . .;
   PROCEDURE N1; . . .;

   . . .
   PROCEDURE Nm; . . .;
BEGIN
   Get_Symbol;
   N0;
END.
```

Fig. 4.2. Recursive descent parser structure

Suppose that the grammar is given by a syntax graph. We can then say that each syntax graph can be seen as the flow diagram of the according procedure. In analogy to the rules for the transformation of BNF into syntax graphs (cf. Chapter 2) there are some rules how to map syntax graphs onto programs. These rules are as follows (where $P(S_i)$ reflects the source code belonging to subgraph S_i):

M1.   A syntax graph representing alternatives, i.e. a graph of the form

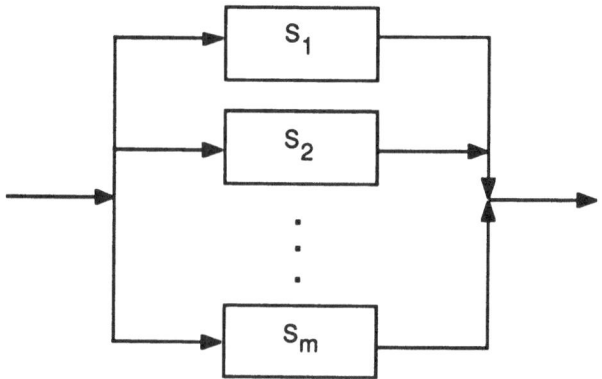

is mapped onto a conditional statement:

```
IF   ch IN FIRST(S1)   THEN   P(S1)   ELSE
     IF   ch IN FIRST(S2)   THEN   P(S2)   ELSE
     . . .
     IF   ch IN FIRST(Sm)   THEN   P(Sm)   ELSE
     Error;
```

M2.   Each graph of the form

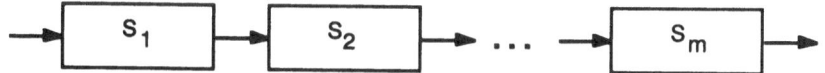

is mapped onto a linear sequence of procedure calls:

```
BEGIN   P(S1);   P(S2);   . . . ;   P(Sm)   END;
```

M3.   Each graph of the form

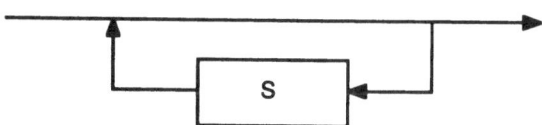

is transformed into a repeat statement:

WHILE   ch **IN** FIRST(S)   **DO**   P(S);

M4.   Each graph of the form

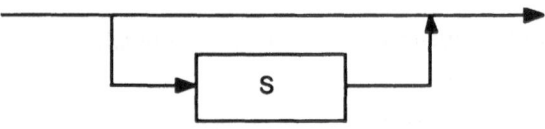

is transformed into a conditional statement.

IF   ch **IN** FIRST(S)   **THEN**   P(S);

M5.   Each graph of the form

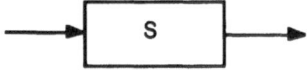

is transformed into a procedure call P(S).

M6.   Each reference to a terminal symbol t

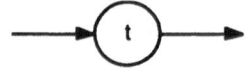

is mapped onto a conditional read statement:

IF   ch = 't'   **THEN**   read(ch)   **ELSE**   Error;

We now develop a recursive descent parser for a grammar G_6 which is a part of the grammar for arithmetic expressions in PL/0. Assume G_6 (T_6, N_6, P_6, S_6) is defined as follows:

$$
\begin{array}{lll}
T_6 & = & \{\,id, +, -, {}^*, /, (,)\,\} \\
N_6 & = & \{\,E, T, F\,\} \\
P_6 & = & \{\,E \;\to\; T\ \{(+|\,-)\,T\} \\
& & \phantom{\{}\,T \;\to\; F\ \{({}^*\,|\,/)\,F\} \\
& & \phantom{\{}\,F \;\to\; id\ |\ (E)\,\} \\
S_6 & = & \{\,E\,\}
\end{array}
$$

The appropriate syntax diagrams are shown in Figure 4.3.

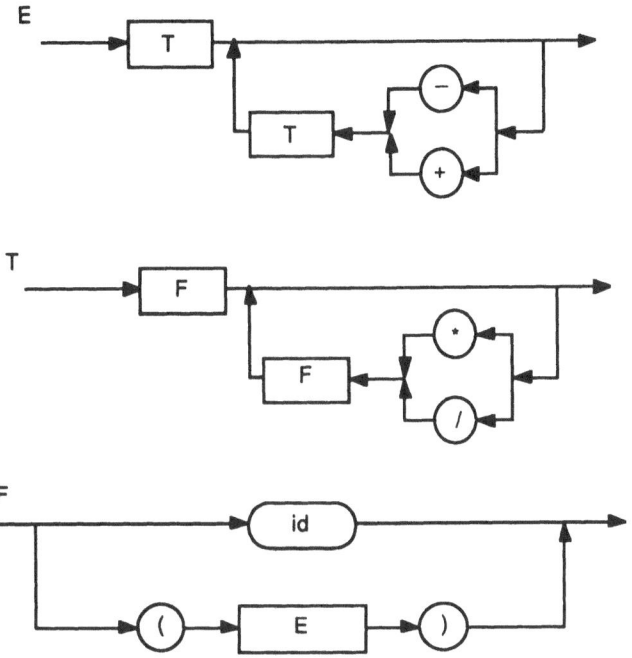

Fig. 4.3.   Syntax graphs for grammar G_6

Before starting to design a recursive descent parser for grammar G_6, we determine the FIRST and FOLLOW sets of the nonterminals of G_6.

Table 4.2.   FIRST and FOLLOW sets of G_6

$X \in N_6$	FIRST (X)	FOLLOW (X)
E	id, (	)
T	id, (	+, -,)
F	id, (	+, -, *, /,)

To prove that G_6 is an LL(1)-grammar we have to show that

$$\text{FIRST(id)} \cap \text{FIRST((E))} = \varnothing$$

because of the last production in P_6. Since

$$\text{FIRST(id)} = \{\, \text{id} \,\} \quad \text{and} \quad \text{FIRST((E))} = \{\, (\, \},$$

these two sets are disjoint. Thus, an analysis with no dead locks will be guaranteed.

```
PROGRAM G6Parser;

  PROCEDURE Error (n: INTEGER);
  BEGIN
    WriteLn;
    WriteString('** Syntactical error occurred, No: ');
    WriteInt(n, 3); WriteLn;
    Halt
  END (* Error *);

  PROCEDURE E;

    PROCEDURE T;

      PROCEDURE F;
      BEGIN (* F *)
        CASE symbol OF
          id  :   Get_Symbol;
        | '(' :   Get_Symbol;   E;
                  IF symbol = ')' THEN Get_Symbol
                  ELSE Error(1) END;
          ELSE    Error(2);
        END;
      END (* F *);

    BEGIN (* T *)
      F;
      WHILE symbol IN ['*', '/'] DO
        Get_Symbol;  F;
      END;
    END (* T *)

  BEGIN (* E *)
    T;
    WHILE symbol IN ['+', '-'] DO
      Get_Symbol;  T;
    END;
  END (* E *);

BEGIN (* G6Parser *)
  Init;    Get_Symbol;    E;
  Halt;
END (* G6Parser *).
```

Fig. 4.4.   Recursive descent parser for grammar G_6

The design of the parser for grammar G_6 is rather simple. Doing this, we use the procedure Get_Symbol which represents the scanner (as described in Chapter 3) and provides the next symbol in the global variable symbol. In addition, we need an Error-procedure which can at this stage be quite simple, i.e. just stops the process in case of an error (error recovery will be discussed later). The principal structure (pseudo-code) of the program G6Parser is given in Figure 4.4.

There exist two additional procedures Init and Halt within the program G6Parser. The first one will initialize the files, while the second one stops the process correctly.

4.1.3 Tabular Parsing

The analyzing method shown in Section 4.1.2 does not depend on the syntax of a given programming language. It is a general way of analyzing and, therefore, it is logical that we can design a general analyzing program, which gets the specific information about the syntax of a given programming language from a so-called *parse table*. The model of tabular parsing is shown in Figure 4.5.

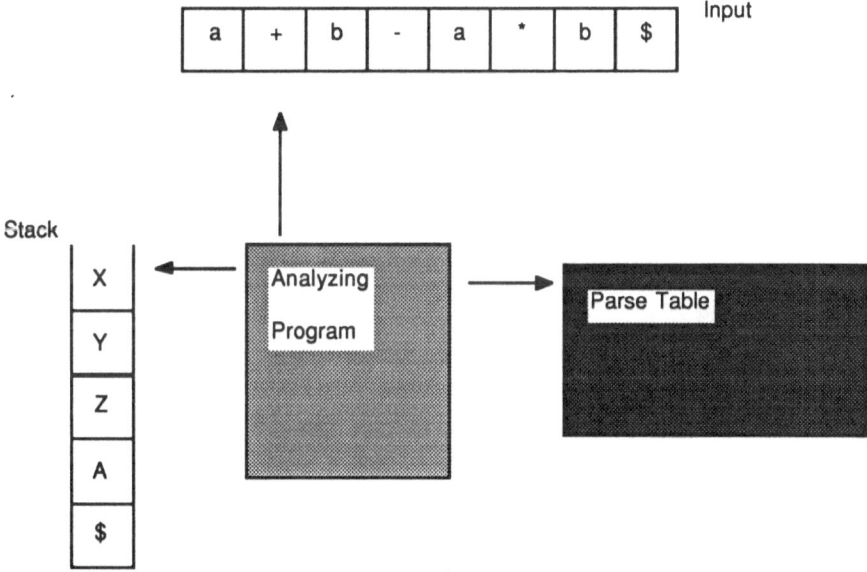

Fig. 4.5. Model of tabular parsing

For tabular parsing we need an input buffer, a stack, and a parse table. The input buffer contains the string which should be analyzed. The input string is followed by a $ indicating the end of the string. The lower end of the stack is also marked with

$. At the beginning, the stack contains just the start symbol of the grammar followed by $.

The parse table is a two-dimensional array $P[N_i, t]$, where N_i is an element of the nonterminals and t is an element of the terminals or $. The endmarker $ is also included in all those FOLLOW(N_i) sets, where N_i occurs on the extreme right-hand side of any sentence that can be derived from the axiom:

$$ \$ \; \in \; \text{FOLLOW}(N_i) \, , \quad \forall N_i \in N : S \xrightarrow{*} \alpha N_i \, . $$

```
(* the stack contains the start symbol and $, the first *)
(* input symbol was read (a), X is top of stack         *)
REPEAT
  IF  X IN T  THEN
    IF  X = a  THEN
       pop X from the stack and read next input character a
    ELSE
       Error . . .;
  ELSE (* X ∈ N *)
    IF  P[X, a] = X → Y₁ Y₂ …Yₘ  THEN
       replace X on top of the stack by Yₘ …Y₂ Y₁
       Y₁ is on top; output X → Y₁ Y₂ …Yₘ
    ELSE (* P[X, a] is empty *)
       Error . . .;
UNTIL  (X = $) AND (a = $);
```

Fig. 4.6.   LL-parse algorithm using a parse table and a stack

An element of the parse table is either empty or it contains a production of the grammar. The analyzing program is now controlled by the current input symbol (a) and the symbol on top of the stack (X) as follows:

1. If $X = a = \$$, the parser accepts the input string and stops.

2. If $X = a \neq \$$, the parser pops X off the stack and reads the next input character.

3. If $X \in T$ and $X \neq a$ or $X \in N$ and $P[X, a]$ is empty, the parser calls an error recovery procedure, because a syntax error occurred.

4. If $X \in N$ and $P[X, a] = X \to Y_1 Y_2 ... Y_m$, where $Y_i \in (N \cup T)$, and $i = 1, 2, ..., m$, the parser replaces X on top of the stack by $Y_m ... Y_2 Y_1$ with Y_1 on top. In this case, the parser has the production $X \to Y_1 Y_2 ... Y_m$ as an output.

The parser's behaviour can also be described using the algorithm of Figure 4.6, while the construction of a parse table is demonstrated by the algorithm given in Figure 4.7.

```
FOR   { ∀ (N → σ) ∈ P }   DO

   FOR   { ∀ t ∈ T : t ∈ FIRST(σ) }   DO
      add N → σ to P[N, t];

   IF  { σ →* ε }   THEN
      FOR   { ∀ x ∈ FOLLOW(N) }   DO
         add N → σ to P[N, x];
   END;

END;
```

Fig. 4.7.   Algorithm to construct a LL-parse table

The idea of the algorithm is the following [AHOS 86]: Suppose $N \to \sigma$ is a production and $t \in$ FIRST(σ). Then, the parser will replace N by σ when the current input symbol is t. A problem occurs in the following situation: $\sigma = \varepsilon$ or $\sigma \to^* \varepsilon$. In this case, we should again replace N by σ, if the current input symbol is an element of FOLLOW(N), or if the $ on the input has been reached and $ is in FOLLOW(N).

This algorithm generates just one entry for each position of the parse table when considering an LL(1)-grammar. The proof is simple: Assume that the algorithm generates more than one entry for an element P [N, t], e.g.

$P[N, t] = \{ N \to \sigma_i, N \to \sigma_j \mid i \neq j \}$.

Then, there must either exist a production $N \to \sigma_i \mid \sigma_j$, where

$FIRST(\sigma_i) \cap FIRST(\sigma_j) = \{ t \} \neq \varnothing$,

which is a contradiction to characteristic C1, or a left-recursive production $N \to N\sigma$ of a nonterminal N that can be derived to the empty string ($N\sigma \to^* \varepsilon$), where

$FIRST(N) \cap FOLLOW(N) = \{ t \} \neq \varnothing$,

which is a contradiction to characteristic C2. Thus, a grammar is not LL(1), if the algorithm of Figure 4.7 produces more than one entry for a parse table.

To give an example for the construction and usage of a parse table we modify our grammar G_0 (T_0, N_0, P_0, S_0) to grammar G_7 (T_7, N_7, P_7, S_7) as follows:

T_7 = { id, +, -, *, /, (,) }

N_7 = {EXPR, E, TERM, T, FACTOR}

P_7 = { EXPR   →   TERM E

TERM   →   FACTOR T

FACTOR →   id | (EXPR)

E   →   + TERM E | - TERM E | ε

T   →   * FACTOR T | / FACTOR T | ε }

S_7 = { EXPR }

The FIRST and FOLLOW sets for grammar G_7 are given in Table 4.3, while Table 4.4 shows the appropriate parse table.

Table 4.3.   FIRST and FOLLOW sets of G_7

σ	FIRST (σ)	FOLLOW (σ)
id	id	undefined
+	+	undefined
-	-	undefined
*	*	undefined
/	/	undefined
(	(	undefined
)	)	undefined
EXPR	id, (	)
E	+, -, ε	), $
TERM	id, (	), +, -
T	*, /, ε	), +, -, $
FACTOR	id, (	), +, -, *, /

Table 4.4.   Parse table for grammar G_7

	id	+	-	*	/	(	)	$
EXPR	TERM E					TERM E		
E		+ TERM E	- TERM E				ε	ε
TERM	FACTOR T					FACTOR T		
T		ε	ε	* FACTOR T	/ FACTOR T		ε	ε
FACTOR	id					(EXPR)		

To exemplify the LL-parsing algorithm of Figure 4.6, we consider the input string

id + id - id * id$

and find the parser making the steps shown in Figure 4.8.

stack	input	output
$ EXPR	id + id - id * id $	
$ E TERM	id + id - id * id $	EXPR → TERM E
$ E T FACTOR	id + id - id * id $	TERM → FACTOR T
$ E T id	id + id - id * id $	FACTOR → id
$ E T	+ id - id * id $	
$ E	+ id - id * id $	T → ε
$ E TERM +	+ id - id * id $	E → + TERM E
$ E TERM	id - id * id $	
$ E T FACTOR	id - id * id $	TERM → FACTOR T
$ E T id	id - id * id $	FACTOR → id
$ E T	- id * id $	
$ E	- id * id $	T → ε
$ E TERM -	- id * id $	E → - TERM E
$ E TERM	id * id $	
$ E T FACTOR	id * id $	TERM → FACTOR T
$ E T id	id * id $	FACTOR → id
$ E T	* id $	
$ E T FACTOR *	* id $	T → * FACTOR T
$ E T FACTOR	id $	
$ E T id	id $	FACTOR → id
$ E T	$	
$ E	$	T → ε
$	$	E → ε

Fig. 4.8. Steps made by the parser on input id + id - id*id$

Reading the stack column from top to bottom we can recognize the leftmost derivation of the input sentence. Thus, we are able to recognize the correlation between
top-down parsing, leftmost derivations (as introduced in Chapter 2) and the usage
of a stack.

4.2   Bottom-up Analysis

Like LL-grammars for top-down analysis we introduce LR-grammars in an informal way before starting to explain the principles of bottom-up analysis (shift-reduce analysis) and to introduce LR-parsers and the generation of SLR parser tables (Section 4.2.3).

4.2.1   LR(k)-grammars

Context-free LR(k)-grammars are the largest class of grammars which can be parsed bottom-up. The "L" of LR(k) means that the input will be read from left to right, while the "R" indicates rightmost derivations. The "k" stands for a look ahead of k symbols.

We start with the fundamental definition of a *handle*. In general, we can say that a string's substring is called a handle, if it can be reduced using the left side of an appropriate production, provided that the reduction corresponds to a step in the leftmost reduction of the string to the grammar's start symbol. Thus, a handle can be said to be representing a particular reduction step (or derivation step, depending on the point of view). Clearly, handles (and therefore those reduction steps) can be recognized by the parsing technique which will be introduced later in this Chapter.

Now, a more formal definition of a handle is given as follows: Let G (N, T, P, S) be a context-free grammar and suppose that

$$S \quad \rightarrow^* \quad \alpha X t \quad \rightarrow \quad \alpha \beta t$$

is a rightmost derivation (where $t \in T^*$). Then, we call β at the given position a *handle* of $\alpha \beta t$.

Thus, a substring β of a string $\alpha \beta t$ is said to be a handle if

$$\alpha \beta t \quad \leftarrow \quad \alpha X t$$

is the leftmost reduction.

The processing of a sentence using leftmost reductions can be handled very well when using a stack mechanism. Then, the handle will always be on top of stack. Considering once again grammar G_0 (N_0, T_0, P_0, S_0), we are able to exemplify this as follows (where the changes on top of the stack are caused either by pushing input symbols on the stack or by reducing a handle on top of the stack):

	input	stack
0	x + y - x	
1	x + y - x	**x**
2	+ y - x	**FACTOR**
3	+ y - x	**TERM**
4	+ y - x	EXPR
5	y - x	EXPR +
6	- x	EXPR + **y**
7	- x	EXPR + **FACTOR**
8	- x	**EXPR + TERM**
9	- x	EXPR
10	x	EXPR -
11		EXPR - **x**
12		EXPR - **FACTOR**
13		**EXPR - TERM**
14		EXPR

Here, the handle is bold faced. Reading the stack column from bottom to top we can recognize the rightmost derivation of the given sentence:

EXPR	$\rightarrow$	EXPR - TERM
	$\rightarrow$	EXPR - FACTOR
	$\rightarrow$	EXPR - x
	$\rightarrow$	EXPR + TERM - x
	$\rightarrow$	EXPR + FACTOR - x
	$\rightarrow$	EXPR + y - x
	$\rightarrow$	TERM + y - x
	$\rightarrow$	FACTOR + y - x
	$\rightarrow$	x + y - x

The main actions using a stack are *shifting* and *reducing*, as shown in the example given above. This means, that one symbol from the input buffer is shifted onto the stack and if it is a handle, it will be reduced to a nonterminal (i.e. the handle is replaced by the left side of an appropriate production).

Now, we define an LR(k)-grammar in the following (informal) way: A grammar is said to be an *LR(k)-grammar*, if it is always possible to determine the handle uniquely in consideration of the current stack contents, and the next k input characters (i.e. that there will occur no shift-reduce and no reduce-reduce conflicts, as we will see later). The cases k = 0 and k = 1 are of practical interest.

LR(k)-grammars are *unambiguous*, otherwise it would not be possible to determine a handle uniquely. The proof is simple. We assume that G (N, T, P, S) is LR(k), for some k ≥ 0, and that w ∈ L (G). If

$$S \xrightarrow{*} w \quad = \quad S \to \sigma_1 \to \sigma_2 \to \dots \to \sigma_{m-1} \to \sigma_m = w$$

is a rightmost derivation of w, then σ_{m-1} is unique since it corresponds to a uniquely determined handle (cf. the example above). In other words, if

$$S \to \tau_1 \to \tau_2 \to \dots \to \tau_{n-1} \to \tau_n = w$$

is a derivation according to G, then $\tau_{n-1} = \sigma_{m-1}$. Similarly, we conclude that the uniqueness of σ_k implies the uniqueness σ_{k-1}, for k = m, m-1, ... , 2. Therefore, only one rightmost derivation of w exists and by that only one syntax tree and consequently only one leftmost derivation.

It can be shown that every LL(k)-grammar is also an LR(k)-grammar and that for every LR(k)-grammar with k > 1 an equivalent LR(1)-grammar exists (see for example [WAIT 84] or [SALO 73]).

4.2.2 Shift-Reduce Analysis

As we already know, bottom-up parsing means to generate a parse tree for a given input starting at the leaves and working up to the root of the tree. This is equivalent to the leftmost reduction (or the rightmost derivation) of a sentence $\alpha \in T^*$ to the start symbol S of the considered grammar:

$$\alpha \xleftarrow{*} S .$$

To exemplify the process we consider grammar G_8 (T_8, N_8, P_8, S_8):

$$
\begin{array}{lll}
T_8 & = & \{\, x1, x2, x3, x4, x5, ",", :, \text{INTEGER} \,\} \\
N_8 & = & \{\, S, \text{VarList}, \text{Var} \,\} \\
P_8 & = & \{\ (1)\ \ S \qquad\qquad \to \qquad \text{VarList} : \text{INTEGER} \\
& & \quad\ (2)\ \ \text{VarList} \qquad \to \qquad \text{VarList} , \text{Var} \mid \text{Var} \\
& & \quad\ (3)\ \ \text{Var} \qquad\qquad \to \qquad x1 \mid x2 \mid x3 \mid x4 \mid x5 \,\} \\
S_8 & = & \{\, S \,\}
\end{array}
$$

Grammar G_8 allows the generation of sentences representing the declaration of integer variables in a PASCAL-like notation. The sentence

x1, x2, x3 : INTEGER

belongs to the language L (G_8) and it can be reduced to the start symbol by the following set of leftmost reductions:

x1, x2, x3 : INTEGER	←	**Var**, x2, x3 : INTEGER
	←	VarList, **x2**, x3 : INTEGER
	←	**VarList, Var**, x3 : INTEGER
	←	VarList, **x3** : INTEGER
	←	**VarList, Var** : INTEGER
	←	**VarList : INTEGER**
	←	S

In each step of the leftmost reduction given above, the handle is bold faced. As we have already mentioned, the analysis of a sentence using leftmost reductions can be implemented using a stack. The idea is then that the sentence which should be analyzed is shifted from an input buffer step by step onto the stack. Previous to each shift operation it is verified whether a handle is on top of the stack which can be reduced using the left side of a production. The input will be accepted, if the input buffer is empty and the axiom of the grammar is on top of the stack. The principal algorithm is given in Figure 4.9.

```
(* Assumptions: stack is empty and read-pointer is  *)
(*              on first input symbol                *)

Shift;  (* get first input symbol on stack *)

REPEAT
  IF  Handle_on_Top_of_Stack  THEN
    Reduce  (* replace top of stack by the left  *)
            (* side of a production              *)
  ELSE
    Shift   (* get next input symbol on stack    *)
  END;
UNTIL  Input_Empty AND No_Handle_on_Top_of_Stack;

IF  Axiom_on_Top_of_Stack  THEN
  Accept    (* input was syntactically correct   *)
ELSE
  Reject    (* input was syntactically incorrect *)
END;
```

Fig. 4.9. Algorithm for shift-reduce analysis

We call this analysis *shift-reduce analysis* since the shift and reduce actions are characteristic of this analysis. Figure 4.10 shows for the reductions of the sentence

x1, x2, x3 : INTEGER ,

the respective stack contents, and the executed actions (where reduce(i) means that the top of the stack will be replaced by the left side of production i).

input	stack	action
x1, x2, x3 : INTEGER $		shift
, x2, x3 : INTEGER $	x1	reduce (3)
, x2, x3 : INTEGER $	Var	reduce (2)
, x2, x3 : INTEGER $	VarList	shift
x2, x3 : INTEGER $	VarList ,	shift
, x3 : INTEGER $	VarList , x2	reduce (3)
, x3 : INTEGER $	VarList , Var	reduce (2)
, x3 : INTEGER $	VarList	shift
x3 : INTEGER $	VarList ,	shift
: INTEGER $	VarList , x3	reduce (3)
: INTEGER $	VarList , Var	reduce (2)
: INTEGER $	VarList	shift
INTEGER $	VarList :	shift
$	VarList : INTEGER	reduce (1)
$	S	*accept*

Fig. 4.10. Shift-reduce analysis using a stack

Now, reading the stack column from bottom to top we can recognize the rightmost derivation of the input sentence.

4.2.3   LR-Parser

The principle of bottom-up parsing was introduced in Section 4.2.2, but we did not explain how to decide, whether to shift or to reduce in a specific situation (i.e. we gave no idea, how a handle can be recognized). For this decision process we use *tables* similar to the tabular top-down parsing. The general model of tabular parsing as given in Figure 4.5 is refined for LR-parsing. The model of an LR-parser consists of an analysing program and an input buffer (similar to the representations in section 4.1.3). But the parse table is split up into

- an *action-table* and

- a *goto-table*,

and the stack contains not only symbols of the grammar (X_i), but also states (s_i) indicating the contents of the stack. The refined model is given in Figure 4.11.

The state on top of the stack, together with the current input symbol, determines the above-mentioned decision process, i.e. these two index the parse table. Each state in the stack reflects uniquely the proceeding analysis process. Thus, LR-parsing uses much more information than tabular LL-parsing, that is to say not only the element on top of stack and the next input symbol, but all the information about the preceding parse process and the next input symbol(s).

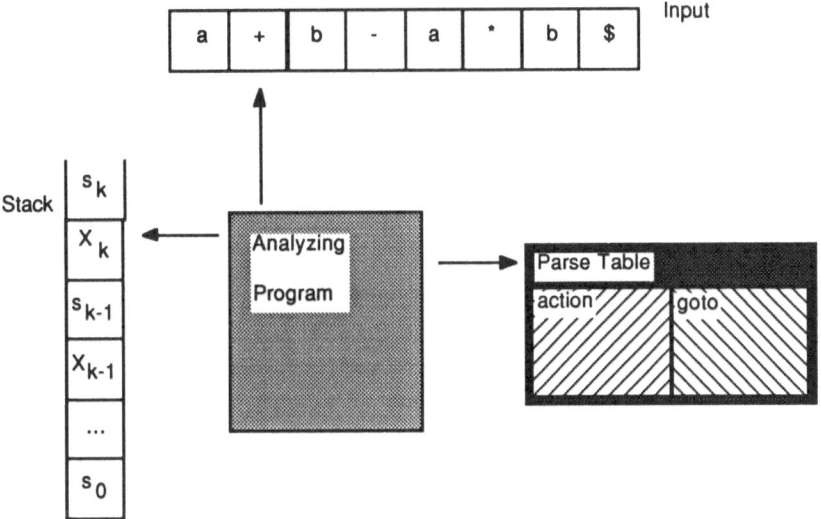

Fig. 4.11. Model of LR-parsing

As we have already seen when discussing the general shift-reduce analysis, the principal actions of the parser or analyzing program are:

- *shift*, i.e. the next input symbol will be shifted on the stack and depending on that symbol and the current stack a new state will get on top of the stack;

- *reduce*, i.e. a handle is recognized (considering the current input symbol and the state on top of the stack) and is reduced using the left side of a production. Depending on that symbol and the current state a new state will get on top of the stack;

- *accept*, i.e. the input will be accepted when the end of the input ($) is reached and a final state is on top of the stack;

- *error*, otherwise.

These actions of the parser are supported by the parse table, i.e. the *action-table* and the *goto-table*. The two-dimensional action-table has entries for pairs (s_i, t_j), where t_j is a terminal and s_i is a state of the stack. Thus, when having state s_k on top of stack and t_m as current input symbol the analyzing program will consult the action-table $A(s_k, t_m)$ to decide about the next analyzing step in the following way:

If $A(s_k, t_m)$ is a state s_i (i.e. shift s_i) of the stack, then when scanning symbol t_m in state s_k, t_m will be pushed onto the stack and after that state s_i will get top of stack.

If $A(s_k, t_m)$ is a production (i.e. reduce with production p_i) of the grammar $(X \rightarrow \alpha)$, then when scanning symbol t_m in state s_k, a handle is recognized and will be reduced using the given production, i.e. 2 * length(handle) pops will be put on the stack, so that state s_j is now on top of the stack. Now, the left side of the production (say X) which is used to reduce the handle is shifted onto the stack and the new state on top of the stack will be determined by consulting the goto-table $G(s_j, X)$.

Thus, the elements of the goto-table are states which are placed on top of stack when a specific nonterminal is in a certain state pushed on the stack.

If $A(s_k, t_m)$ is accept then the analysis process can stop and the input was correct, i.e. will be accepted.

If $A(s_k, t_m)$ contains no entry then an error occurred, i.e. the input is incorrect and will not be accepted.

The principal algorithm is given in Figure 4.12. To exemplify the algorithm of Figure 4.12 we consider the *augmented grammar* G_8 which is extended by the production $S' \rightarrow S$. Using this additional production, the acceptance of an input sentence can be uniquely determined, i.e. an input will be accepted if and only if the parser reduces with this additional production. The grammar is given in the following only by the set of productions (the productions are numbered for reference in the action-table):

(0)	S'	$\rightarrow$	S
(1)	S	$\rightarrow$	VarList : INTEGER
(2)	VarList	$\rightarrow$	VarList , Var
(3)	VarList	$\rightarrow$	Var
(4)	Var	$\rightarrow$	x1
(5)	Var	$\rightarrow$	x2
(6)	Var	$\rightarrow$	x3
(7)	Var	$\rightarrow$	x4
(8)	Var	$\rightarrow$	x5

The action- and goto-table are given in Figure 4.13 (the construction of these tables will be explained later).

```
(* init. state on stack, 1st input sym. is next to read *)
WHILE  A[top_of_stack, current_input] ≠ accept  DO
  IF  A[top_of_stack, current_input] = shift(s)  THEN
    push(current_input);
    push(s);  (* s is new top of stack *)
    INC(read_pointer);
  ELSIF  A[top_of_stack, current_input] = reduce(p)  THEN
                   (* p is the number of a production *)
    h := length(handle);
    FOR  i := 1  TO  2*h  DO  pop(...);
                   (* pop h symbols of the grammar *)
                   (*   and h states off the stack *)
    s := G[top_of_stack, left_side(p)];
                   (* get the new top of stack    *)
                   (* from the goto-table         *)
    push(left_side(p));
    push(s);
  ELSIF  A[top_of_stack, current_input] = empty  THEN
    Error(...);
  END;
END;
```

Fig. 4.12. Algorithm for LR-parsing

| | Action-table | | | | | | | | | Goto-table | | |
states	x1	x2	x3	x4	x5	,	:	INT	$	S	VarL	Var
s0	s4	s5	s6	s7	s8					s1	s2	s3
s1									acc			
s2						s10	s9					
s3						p3	p3					
s4						p4	p4					
s5						p5	p5					
s6						p6	p6					
s7						p7	p7					
s8						p8	p8					
s9								s11				
s10	s4	s5	s6	s7	s8							s12
s11									p1			
s12						p2	p2					

Fig. 4.13. Action and goto-table for the augmented grammar G_8

The coding of the tables given in Figure 4.13 is as follows: s_i means that the shift operation described above will be executed with state i (except for those s_i in the leftmost column, of course), p_i means that a reduction using production p_i will be performed, acc stands for accept, INT stands for INTEGER, and VarL for VarList.

Now, the analysis of the sentence x1, x2, x3: INTEGER will be given as follows (the stack is assumed to be initialized by $ s0):

input	stack	action / reduction
x1, x2, x3 : INTEGER $	$ s0	shift
, x2, x3 : INTEGER $	$ s0 x1 s4	x1 ← Var
, x2, x3 : INTEGER $	$ s0 V s3	Var ← VarList
, x2, x3 : INTEGER $	$ s0 VL s2	shift
x2, x3 : INTEGER $	$ s0 VL s2 , s10	shift
, x3 : INTEGER $	$ s0 VL s2 , s10 x2 s5	x2 ← Var
, x3 : INTEGER $	$ s0 VL s2 , s10 V s12	VarList, Var ← VarList
, x3 : INTEGER $	$ s0 VL s2	shift
x3 : INTEGER $	$ s0 VL s2 , s10	shift
: INTEGER $	$ s0 VL s2 , s10 x3 s6	x3 ← Var
: INTEGER $	$ s0 VL s2 , s10 V s12	VarList, Var ← VarList
: INTEGER $	$ s0 VL s2	shift
INTEGER $	$ s0 VL s2 : s9	shift
$	$ s0 VL s2 : s9 INT s11	VarList : INTEGER ← S
$	$ s0 S s1	*accept*

Fig. 4.14. LR-parsing based on the parse tables

Once again, when reading the stack column from bottom to top (top to bottom) we can recognize the rightmost derivation (leftmost reduction) of the input sentence. Hence, the relation between bottom-up parse tree generation and the stack implementation of bottom-up analysis is obvious.

Construction of the parse tables

Constructing parse tables is a very complex process and would not be done manually even for grammars consisting of only a few productions, but is done by programs. An example for such an program is Yacc [JOHN 75]. Nevertheless, such programs can only be understood, if one has at least an idea about how to construct *SLR* (*simple LR*) parse tables. Therefore, the construction process of simple LR parse tables will be introduced in the following, while the other methods (i.e. the canonical LR and the look ahead LR or LALR) will not be considered here. For more details about these methods see [AHOS 86], for example.

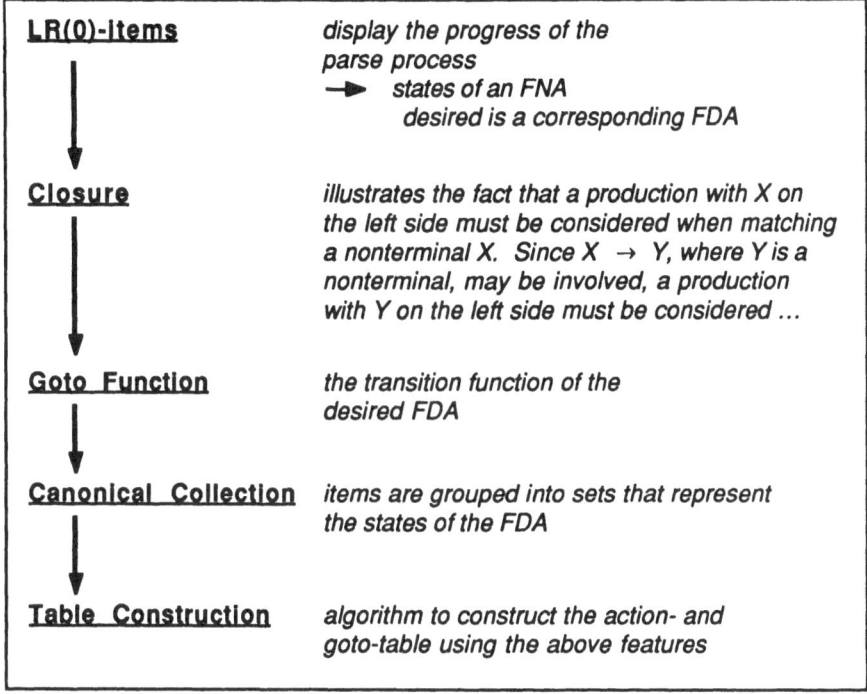

Fig. 4.15. Principal procedure to construct LR-parse tables

The principal procedure for the generation of an action- and a goto-table is shown in Figure 4.15. Each element of Figure 4.15 will be described in the following. First, an indicator is needed to display the progress of the parse process. For this reason *LR(0)-items* are defined (the 0 indicates that no look ahead information is included):

Let $X \rightarrow \sigma_1 \sigma_2$ be a production of a grammar G. An LR(0)-item of grammar G contains a dot (the indicator) at some position of the right side of the productions of G. Thus, the items corresponding to the given production are

$$X \quad \rightarrow \quad \cdot \sigma_1 \sigma_2$$
$$X \quad \rightarrow \quad \sigma_1 \cdot \sigma_2$$
$$X \quad \rightarrow \quad \sigma_1 \sigma_2 \cdot$$

The dot indicates how many symbols of the input are already analyzed. For example, the item

$$\text{VarList} \quad \rightarrow \quad \text{VarList}, \cdot \text{Var}$$

means that in the input a VarList followed by a comma was already recognized and the rest of the input is expected to be derivable from Var.

The LR(0)-items of a grammar can be understood as the states of a finite non-deterministic automaton accepting the contents of the stack during the analyzing process. Now, the idea is to construct a corresponding finite deterministic automaton. This can be done by grouping the LR(0)-items together into sets (i.e. applying the subset construction, cf. Chapter 3). Therefore, a few more definitions will be needed.

A set of LR(0)-items is called a *LR(0)-set*.

Let I be an LR(0)-set. The *closure(I)* is defined by the following algorithm:

```
INCLUDE(I, closure(I));
          (* initializes the closure with the set I *)

REPEAT

  changes := FALSE;
          (* flag to indicate changes of closure(I) *)
  FOR   (∀ (X → α•Yβ) ∈ closure(I))   DO

    FOR   (∀ (Y → γ) ∈ P)   DO
      IF  (γ ∈ N)  THEN  changes := TRUE   END;
          (* γ causes new inclusions
              if it is a nonterminal *)
      INCLUDE(Y → •γ, closure(I));
    END;

  END;

UNTIL NOT changes;
```

Fig. 4.16. Algorithm for generating the closure of a LR(0)-set

Consider grammar G_8 and the LR(0)-item

  VarList   →   VarList , • Var

then

$$\text{closure(VarList} \rightarrow \text{VarList}, \cdot \text{Var}) = \{ \quad \begin{array}{lll} \text{VarList} & \rightarrow & \text{VarList}, \cdot \text{Var} \\ \text{Var} & \rightarrow & \cdot \text{x1} \\ \text{Var} & \rightarrow & \cdot \text{x2} \\ \text{Var} & \rightarrow & \cdot \text{x3} \\ \text{Var} & \rightarrow & \cdot \text{x4} \\ \text{Var} & \rightarrow & \cdot \text{x5} \ \} \,. \end{array}$$

Let β be an element of V and I be an LR(0)-set. Then, *goto(I, β)* is defined as

$$\text{goto } (I, \beta) \quad = \quad \text{closure } (I')$$

where $I' = \{ N \rightarrow \alpha \beta \cdot \gamma \mid (N \rightarrow \alpha \cdot \beta \gamma) \in I \}$. The transition function of the desired finite automaton is described by goto(I, β), i.e. goto defines a transition from one state into another state when scanning the symbol β.

Let us assume I to be the closure(VarList $\rightarrow$ VarList, $\cdot$ Var) and β to be x1. Then,

$$I' \quad = \quad \{ N \rightarrow \alpha \, \text{x1} \cdot \gamma \mid (N \rightarrow \alpha \cdot \text{x1} \, \gamma) \in I \} \quad = \quad \{ \text{Var} \rightarrow \text{x1} \cdot \}$$

and

$$\text{goto}(I, \beta) \quad = \quad \text{closure}(I') \quad = \quad \{ \text{Var} \rightarrow \text{x1} \cdot \} \,.$$

Items can now be grouped together into sets representing the states of the desired finite deterministic automaton. Therefore, we construct the so-called *canonical collection C* of LR(0)-sets using the algorithm given in Figure 4.17 for an augmented grammar G.

```
INCLUDE(closure(S' → •S), C);
        (* initializes the canonical collection C *)

REPEAT
  changes := FALSE;
  FOR   ( ∀ LR(0)-sets I ∈ C )  DO
    FOR   ( ∀ β ∈ V )  DO
      IF  (goto(I,β) ≠ ∅) AND (goto(I,β) ∉ C)   THEN
        INCLUDE(goto(I,β), C);
        changes := TRUE;
      END;
    END;
  END;
UNTIL NOT changes;
```

Fig. 4.17. Construction of the canonical collection C of LR(0)-sets

Considering once more the augmented grammar G_8, the algorithm of Figure 4.17 defines the following canonical collection C of LR(0)-sets (using the abbreviations VL for VarList, V for Var, and INT for INTEGER).

I_0 =   closure(S' → •S)   = { S' → •S

                                      S → •VL : INT

                                    VL → •VL , V

                                    VL → •V

                                    V → •x1

                                    V → •x2

                                    V → •x3

                                    V → •x4

                                    V → •x5 }

I_1 = goto(I_0,S)   = closure(S' → S•)   = { S' → S• }

I_2 = goto(I_0,VL)   = closure(S → VL• : INT

                              VL → VL• , V) = { S   → VL• : INT

                                            VL → VL• , V }

I_3 = goto(I_0,V)   = closure(VL → V•)   = { VL → V• }

I_4 = goto(I_0,x1)   = closure(V → x1•)   = { V → x1• }

I_5 = goto(I_0,x2)   = closure(V → x2•)   = { V → x2• }

I_6 = goto(I_0,x3)   = closure(V → x3•)   = { V → x3• }

I_7 = goto(I_0,x4)   = closure(V → x4•)   = { V → x4• }

I_8 = goto(I_0,x5)   = closure(V → x5•)   = { V → x5• }

I_9 = goto(I_2,:)   = closure(S → VL : •INT) = { S   → VL : • INT }

I_{10} = goto(I_2,",")   = closure(VL → VL , •V) = { VL → VL , • V

                                          V → •x1

                                          V → •x2

                                          V → •x3

                                          V → •x4

                                          V → •x5 }

I_{11} = goto(I_9,INT)   = closure(S → VL : INT•) = { S → VL : INT• }

I_{12} = goto(I_{10},V)   = closure(VL → VL , V•) = { VL → VL , V• }

Each I_k ($0 \le k \le 12$, for the given example) represents a state of the desired finite deterministic automaton. Thus, the canonical collection is characterized by the set of all I_k. In the example considered, the automaton consists of 13 states. This set is complete because all other goto(I_k, β) are either empty or already an element of the collection. The corresponding automaton is shown in Figure 4.18.

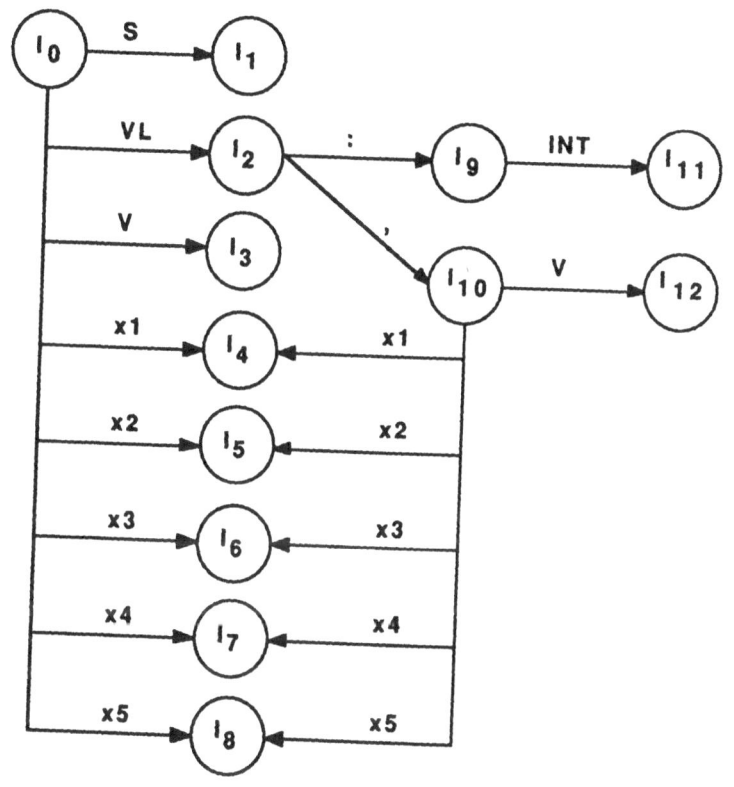

Fig. 4.18. Transition diagram representing the goto-function

Finally, the parsing tables can be constructed. The construction process assumes an augmented grammar, i.e. the grammar is extended by a new start symbol S' and a new production S' → S. Then,

- we have to calculate the FOLLOW-sets for each nonterminal of the grammar, and

- we have to construct the canonical collection C of LR(0)-sets.

Each state of our finite deterministic automaton corresponds to one of the sets I_k in the canonical collection. Now, the algorithm for the entries in the action- and goto-table is given in Figure 4.19.

```
FOR  i := 0  TO  n  DO
        (* the canonical collection consists of n+1 sets *)

    (* ACTION-table : *)

    FOR  m := 1  TO  k  DO
            (* the grammar consists of k terminal symbols *)
        IF  ((X → α•t_mβ) ∈ I_i) AND (goto(I_i,t_m) = I_j)  THEN
            A(s_i,t_m) := shift(j)
        END
    END;

    FOR  (∀(X → α•) ∈ I_i)  DO
        FOR  m := 1  TO  k  DO
            IF  (t_m ∈ FOLLOW(X))  THEN
                A(s_i,t_m) := reduce(p);
                (* where p is the number of the production *)
                (* X → α in the grammar *)
            END
        END
    END;

    IF  ((S' → S•) ∈ I_i)  THEN
        A(s_i,$) := accept;
    END;

    (* GOTO-table : *)

    FOR  (∀ X ∈ N)  DO
        IF  (goto(I_i,X) = I_j)  THEN
            G(s_i,X) = shift(j);
        END
    END

END;
```

Fig. 4.19. Algorithm for constructing the action- and goto-table

The action- and goto-table of Figure 4.13 can then be generated using the algorithm of Figure 4.19. To conclude this section, it should be pointed out once more that the LR-parsing methods - especially the generation of the parse tables - are difficult, faulty, and very time consuming to produce manually. Therefore, parser-generating programs are used for LR-parsing.

4.3   Recursive Descent Parser for PL/0

The aim of this section is to give an idea how to implement a simple compiler for a programming language. For this reason, the easy to understand method of *recursive descent parsing* is applied to *PL/0*. Source code for a bottom-up analysis will *not* be given here because it requires not only the code for the compiler itself, but also for the generation of the parser tables. Such a system would be much more complex than the one introduced here and, therefore, probably boring for the reader of this introductory book.

The comments on recursive descent parsing in Chapter 4.1 show that we have to make sure that the grammar for PL/0 as given in Chapter 2.5 is an LL(1)-grammar. This can be proven easily and will be a good exercise for the reader. The FIRST and FOLLOW-sets for the PL/0-grammar are given in Table 4.5 ([WIRT 86]).

Table 4.5.   FIRST and FOLLOW-sets for PL/0

N	FIRST (N)	FOLLOW (N)
BLOCK	const var procedure ident if call begin while	. ;
STATEMENT	ident call begin if while ε	. ; end
CONDITION	odd + - (ident number	then do
EXPRESSION	+ - (ident number	. ; end then do =) >= > <= < #
TERM	(ident number	. ; end then do =) >= > <= < # + -
FACTOR	(ident number	. ; end then do =) >= > <= < # + - * /

A rudimentary program segment representing a recursive descent parser for the programming language PL/0 is following below. The program is based on the lexical analysis as introduced in Chapter 3 (Get_Symbol) and uses the procedures Error(...) and Init which are obvious and, therefore, not described here.

```
PROGRAM Parser;

CONST
     as = 101;    (* size of hash table *)
     cmax = 10;      (* size of var names *)
     BinShift = 16; (* used in hash function *)

TYPE
     alfa = ARRAY [1..cmax] OF CHAR;
     object = (constobj, varobj, procobj);
     symbols = (nul, ident, number, plus, minus, times, slash,
               oddsym, eql, neq, lss, leq, gtr, geq, lparen,
               rparen, comma, semicolon, period, becomes,
               beginsym, endsym, ifsym, thensym, whilesym,
               dosym, callsym, constsym, varsym, procsym);
     symset = SET OF symbols;
     HT_Entry = ^Hash_SymTab;
     Hash_SymTab = RECORD
                     name : alfa;
                     next_name : HT_Entry;
                     CASE kind : object OF
                         constobj : (val : INTEGER);
                         varobj : (level, addr, size : INTEGER);
                         procobj :(level, addr, size : INTEGER);
                     END;

VAR
     symbol : symbols;
     id : alfa;
     num : INTEGER;
     HElement : Hash_SymTab;
     symtable : ARRAY [1..as] OF HT_Entry;

PROCEDURE Hash (vn: alfa): INTEGER;
VAR   lvn : INTEGER;
BEGIN
  lvn := length(vn);
  Hash := (ORD(vn[1]) + ORD(vn[lvn]) + BinShift*lvn) MOD as + 1;
END Hash;
```

```
PROCEDURE InsertST (vn: alfa; k: object);
(*   insert an object into symbol table   *)
  PROCEDURE InsN (VAR q: HT_Entry);
  BEGIN
    IF  q = NIL  THEN
      NEW(q);
      WITH  q  DO
        name := id;
        next_name := NIL;
        kind := k;
        IF  kind = constobj  THEN
          val := num
        ELSE
          level := 0;
          addr := 0;
          size := 0
        END
      END;
    ELSE  IF  q^.name <> vn  THEN
      InsN(q^.next_name);
    END
  END InsN;
BEGIN (*InsertST*)
  InsN(symtable[Hash(vn)]);
END InsertST;


PROCEDURE LookupST (VAR p: Hash_SymTab; vn: alfa) : INTEGER;
(*   find id in symbol table   *)
VAR adr : INTEGER;
  PROCEDURE Find (q: HT_Entry): BOOLEAN;
  BEGIN
    IF  q = NIL  THEN
      RETURN FALSE
    ELSE
      IF  q^.name = vn  THEN
        p := q^;
        RETURN TRUE
      ELSE
        RETURN Find(q^.next_name)
      END
    END
  END Find;
```

```
BEGIN (*LookupST*)
  adr := Hash(vn);
  IF  Find(symtable[adr])  THEN
    RETURN adr
  ELSE
    RETURN 0
  END;
END LookupST;


PROCEDURE Block;

  PROCEDURE Constdeclaration;
  BEGIN
    IF  symbol = ident  THEN
      Get_Symbol;
      IF  symbol = eql  THEN
        Get_Symbol;
        IF  symbol = number  THEN
          InsertST(id,constobj);
          Get_Symbol
        ELSE  Error(…)  END;
      ELSE  Error(…)  END;
    ELSE  Error(…)  END;
  END Constdeclaration;

  PROCEDURE Vardeclaration;
  BEGIN
    IF  symbol = ident  THEN
      InsertST(id,varobj);
      Get_Symbol
    ELSE  Error(…)  END;
  END Vardeclaration;

  PROCEDURE Expression;
    PROCEDURE Term;
      PROCEDURE Factor;
      VAR  i: INTEGER;
      BEGIN    (*Factor*)
        CASE symbol OF
          ident :  i := LookupST(HElement,id);
```

```
                        IF  i = 0  THEN  Error(…)
                        ELSE
                          IF  HElement.kind = procobj  THEN
                            Error(…)  END;
                        END;
                        Get_Symbol
          | number:     Get_Symbol;
          | lparen:     Get_Symbol;
                        Expression;
                        IF  symbol=rparen  THEN  Get_Symbol
                        ELSE  Error(…)  END
            ELSE        Error(…)
          END;
        END Factor;

        BEGIN  (*Term*)
          Factor;
          WHILE  symbol IN [times, slash]  DO
            Get_Symbol; Factor
          END
        END Term;

      BEGIN (*Expression*)
        IF  symbol IN [plus, minus]  THEN
          Get_Symbol; Term
        ELSE  Term  END;
        WHILE  symbol IN [plus,minus]  DO  Get_Symbol; Term  END
      END Expression;

PROCEDURE Condition;
BEGIN
  IF  symbol = oddsym  THEN
    Get_Symbol;
    Expression
  ELSE
    Expression;
    IF  symbol IN [eql,neq,lss,leq,gtr,geq]  THEN
      Get_Symbol;
      Expression;
    ELSE  Error(…)  END;
  END
END Condition;
```

```
PROCEDURE Statement;
VAR  i: INTEGER;
BEGIN
  CASE  symbol  OF
    ident :  i := LookupST(HEelement,id);
              IF  i = 0  THEN  Error(…)
              ELSIF  HElement.kind <> varobj  THEN
                Error(…)  END;
              Get_Symbol;
              IF  symbol = becomes  THEN  Get_Symbol
                ELSE  Error(…)  END;
              Expression
  | callsym: Get_Symbol;
              IF  symbol = ident  THEN
                i := LookupST(HElement,id);
                IF  i = 0  THEN  Error(…)
                ELSIF  HElement.kind <> procobj  THEN
                  Error(…)  END;
                Get_Symbol
              ELSE Error(…) END
  | ifsym:    Get_Symbol;
              Condition;
              IF  symbol = thensym  THEN  Get_Symbol
                ELSE  Error(…)  END;
              Statement
  | beginsym:Get_Symbol;
              Statement;
              WHILE  symbol = semicolon  DO
                Get_Symbol; Statement
              END;
              IF  symbol = endsym  THEN  Get_Symbol
                ELSE  Error(…)  END
  | whilesym:Get_Symbol;
              Condition;
              IF  symbol = dosym  THEN  Get_Symbol
                ELSE  Error(…)  END;
              Statement
  END
END Statement;
```

```
BEGIN (*Block*)
  IF  symbol = constsym  THEN
    Get_Symbol;
    Constdeclaration;
    WHILE  symbol = comma  DO
      Get_Symbol; Constdeclaration
    END;
    IF  symbol = semicolon  THEN  Get_Symbol
    ELSE  Error(...)  END;
  END;
  IF  symbol = varsym  THEN
    Get_Symbol;
    Vardeclaration;
    WHILE  symbol = comma  DO
      Get_Symbol; Vardeclaration
    END;
    IF  symbol = semicolon  THEN  Get_Symbol
    ELSE  Error(...)  END
  END;
  WHILE  symbol = procsym  DO
    Get_Symbol;
    IF  symbol = ident  THEN  InsertST(id,procobj);Get_Symbol
    ELSE  Error(...)  END;
    IF  symbol = semicolon  THEN  Get_Symbol
    ELSE  Error(...)  END;
    Block;
    IF  symbol = semicolon  THEN  Get_Symbol
    ELSE  Error(...)  END;
  END;
  Statement;
END Block;


BEGIN (*Parser*)
  Init;
  Get_Symbol;
  Block;
  IF  symbol <> period  THEN  Error(...)  END;
END Parser.
```

5 Semantic and Type Analysis

In Chapter 3 and 4 different analyzing methods have been introduced. All these analyzers (lexical as well as syntax analyzers) are not concerned with the *semantics* or the *meaning* of given programs. A compiler has to check not only the syntactical correctness of a given source code, but also whether the semantics correspond to that of the programming language. This means, that *semantic analysis* has to guarantee that all *context-sensitive rules* of the programming language are considered.

An example of such a context-sensitive rule of a programming language is that in languages like PASCAL or MODULA-2 identifiers have to be declared before they are used. *Symbol tables* are used to check, if an identifier already has been declared, as explained in Chapter 3. Thus, symbol tables and their usage can be seen as a part of the semantic analysis process and, therefore, it is obvious that semantic analysis can be carried out in parallel to syntax analysis (or must be done in parallel at least in certain situations).

In general, the semantic analysis of a compiler uses the information of the syntax analysis in combination with the semantic rules of the programming language to generate an *internal representation* of the source code which is to be compiled. This generation of an internal representation means that the compiler has to interpret the meaning of the source code and, therefore, that the compiler semantically analyzes the syntactical structures of the source code as they are recognized by the scanner and parser. The internal representation is an *intermediate code* which will be passed on to the code generator.

An introduction to intermediate codes is given below before the so-called syntax-directed translation will be introduced.

5.1   Intermediate Codes

The term *intermediate code* indicates a code structure which lies in complexity between high-level language source code and machine code and therefore, intermediate codes can be understood as an interface between the code generator and all the previous phases of the compiler.

Intermediate codes can be regarded as the machine code of an (ideal) hypothetical computer. The usage of such an abstract machine level has the advantage that

- the compiler itself is *independent* of the target machine and by this is more portable, because all the characteristics of the target hardware are considered in the code generator;

- some optimization strategies (e.g. optimizations depending on register allocations) are easier to perform on intermediate code than on source code.

However, the code which can be generated from an intermediate code will be in general less efficient than a directly generated machine code because of the additional translation level.

In the following, three kinds of intermediate code are introduced which are often used in compilers.

Postfix Notation

Postfix notation is a very simple notation which places an operator on the right end of an expression, i.e. directly behind the operands instead of between the operands. For example, the expression

$$x + y - x * y$$

is in postfix notation

$$x y + x y * - ,$$

since xy+ represents the infix expression $x + y$ and xy* represents $x * y$, etc.

Postfix notation is normally used for stack machines since it can be handled very easily using a stack: When scanning a postfix notation from left to right, each time an operand occurs it will be pushed onto the stack. The occurrence of an operator with m operands means that the n-th operand will be found in position m - n below the top of the stack, i.e. the m-th operand is on top of the stack. Then, these operands are popped off the stack and the result of the operation is pushed onto the stack.

For example, assume x to be 1 and y to be 2 in the above given expression which is then evaluated performing the following steps:

1. push(1);

2. push(2);

3. + needs two operands: the two topmost elements are popped off the stack, added, and the result is pushed onto the stack: push(3);

4. push(1);

5. push(2);

6. * needs two operands: the two topmost elements are popped off the stack, multiplied, and the result is pushed onto the stack: push(2);

7. - needs two operands: pop the two topmost elements (i.e. x+y and x*y) off the stack, subtract them, and push the result onto the stack: push(1).

Three-address Code

The most popular code is the so-called *three-address code* (the name is derived from the circumstance that a statement usually consists of three addresses or registers for two operands or arguments and the result). The typical form of three-address code is

>   res   :=   arg1 **op** arg2

where res, arg1, and arg2 can be constants (arg1 and arg2, only) or identifiers as defined by the programmer or compiler defined auxiliary variables, while **op** is an arbitrary operator. Compiler defined auxiliary variables are used to handle more complex expressions containing not only one operator, i.e. multiple operator expressions are split up into a sequence of expressions containing only one operator and operating on auxiliary variables.

Considering the typical form of three-address code given above we can recognize four basic elements: **op**, arg1, arg2, and res which are often represented in the following form:

op	arg1	arg2	res

where arg1, arg2 and res are typically pointers to symbol table entries. In that case, this form is referred to as *quadruple*.

Three-address code as well as the two-address code which is introduced below, allows very simple translation into code for register machines since operands are often the result of previous operations. Then, the references to results of previous operations are given explicitly, while in postfix code such references are given implicitly by the stack.

Assume that **op** can be MUL, ADD, SUB, and STO to represent the operators *, +, -, and :=. Then the statement z := x + y - x*y results in the following three-address code or sequence of quadruples:

1:	ADD	x	y	av1
2:	MUL	x	y	av2
3:	SUB	av1	av2	av3
4:	STO	av3		z

As shown by this example, the result (res) is usually an auxiliary variable (i.e. a temporary variable). The usage of three-address code requires the usage of sophisticated algorithms to manage all the auxiliary variables (this management of names is normally done using the symbol table). However, auxiliary variables can be avoided using *two-address codes*.

Two-address Code

The auxiliary variables in three-address codes are used to store temporarily results which are needed in subsequent statements. The idea now is to avoid these auxiliary variables by referencing the statement whose result would be the auxiliary variable, when using that specific auxiliary variable as an operand (arg1 or arg2). Thus, the res-field of the three-address code is no longer necessary and the fields for arg1 and arg2 can contain both pointers to the symbol table and pointers to the sequence of the two-address statements itself. Then, the principal form of two-address code is given as follows:

op	arg1	arg2

This form is often referred to as *triple*.

Now, the above example z := x + y - x*y will result in the following two-address code:

1:	ADD	x	y
2:	MUL	x	y
3:	SUB	(1)	(2)
4:	STO	(3)	z

where the numbers in parentheses represent pointers into the sequence of the two-address statements.

To clarify the differences between two-address code and three-address code we consider the statement x := r*s + r*t and set the appropriate triples against the quadruples:

	Triples			Quadruples	
(1)	(*, r, s)		(1)	(*, r, s, av1)	
(2)	(*, r, t)		(2)	(*, r, t, av2)	
(3)	(+, (1), (2))		(3)	(+, av1, av2, av3)	
(4)	(:=, (3), x)		(4)	(:=, av3, x, --)	

Other Codes

Another intermediate representation of source code is a parse tree where all the redundant information is eliminated. Such a tree is called an *abstract syntax tree*. Each leaf of an abstract syntax tree represents an operand while the internal nodes represent the operators. A more detailed discussion on abstract syntax trees can be found in [TREM 85] or [FISC 88], for example.

Similar to the postfix notation it is possible to generate the *prefix notation* of an expression. The prefix notation of an expression can be generated by scanning an abstract syntax tree from left to right and printing an operator upon first encountering it, while for postfix notation an operator will be printed upon last encountering it.

The *P-code* [NORI 81] was designed for PASCAL compilers. It is probably the most prominent intermediate code. The so-called P-machine which is the abstract machine reflected by this intermediate code is a simple hypothetical stack computer with five registers and a memory.

Another form of intermediate code which can be found is the so-called *threaded code* [BELL 73]. In threaded code as introduced by Bell - sometimes also called *direct threaded code* - each operation is mapped onto a subroutine call. Therefore, threaded code generates a list of linear addresses for these subroutines.

5.2 Syntax-directed Translation

As already mentioned, semantic analysis can be done in parallel with syntactic analysis, that is to say, each time a syntactic structure, i.e. a production, is recognized by the parser, the semantic analysis can take place. Thus, the actions of the semantic analysis which are attached to the productions are embedded into the parsing process. These *semantic actions* generate intermediate code whenever they are executed. Thus, the syntactic structure of the source code directs the translation into object code or intermediate code which is why we talk about *syntax-directed translation*. Almost all modern compilers are syntax-directed.

Semantic Actions

Semantic actions are associated with the productions of a context-free grammar. They can be seen as a *code fragment* which will be executed when the appropriate production is recognized by the parser.

For example, consider the G_0-production

$$\text{TERM} \quad \rightarrow \quad \text{TERM} * \text{FACTOR} \quad (* \ A \ *)$$

and assume A to be the associated semantic action. Then, considering a

- *bottom-up parser:* A will be executed when TERM * FACTOR is *reduced* to TERM;

- *top-down parser:* A will be executed when TERM or FACTOR is *expanded*.

Translation into Quadruples

The generation of three-address code (quadruples) is exemplified in the following considering grammar G_0 and the shift-reduce analysis of the sentence x + y - x * y. The code fragments representing the semantic actions assume an "infinite" array of auxiliary variables (av[k]), to simplify matters. Therefore, a variable k is incremented when a new auxiliary variable should be used. EPtr, TPtr, and FPtr can be understood as pointers to where the value of an expression, term, etc. can be found (e.g. a pointer to the symbol table). Subscripts are used to distinguish among the multiple occurrences of nonterminals. The procedure CGen outputs a quadruple according to the actual parameters.

Now we give grammar G_0 by its set of productions together with the semantic actions belonging to each production (EXPR, TERM, and FACTOR is abbreviated by E, T, and F):

(1) E $\rightarrow$ T   (* EPtr := TPtr *)

(2) E_1 $\rightarrow$ E_2 + T   (* INC(k);
                        E_1Ptr := av[k];
                        CGen(ADD, E_2Ptr, TPtr, av[k]); *)

(3) E_1 $\rightarrow$ E_2 - T   (* INC(k);
                        E_1Ptr := av[k];
                        CGen(SUB, E_2Ptr, TPtr, av[k]); *)

(4) T $\rightarrow$ F   (* TPtr := FPtr *)

(5) T_1 $\rightarrow$ T_2 * F   (* INC(k);
                        T_1Ptr := av[k];
                        CGen(MUL, T_2Ptr, FPtr, av[k]); *)

(6) T_1 $\rightarrow$ T_2 / F   (* INC(k);
                        T_1Ptr := av[k];
                        CGen(DIV, T_2Ptr, FPtr, av[k]); *)

(7) F $\rightarrow$ x   (* FPtr := x; *)

(8) F $\rightarrow$ y   (* FPtr := y; *)

(9) F $\rightarrow$ (E)   (* FPtr := EPtr; *)

Since grammar G_0 is a part of the grammar which generates the programming language PL/0, the semantic actions shown can be used to generate intermediate code for arithmetic expressions in PL/0 as shown in Figure 5.1.

input	stack	action	code
x + y - x * y $		shift	
+ y - x * y $	x	reduce(7)	
+ y - x * y $	F	reduce(4)	
+ y - x * y $	T	reduce(1)	
+ y - x * y $	E	shift	
y - x * y $	E +	shift	
- x * y $	E + y	reduce(8)	
- x * y $	E + F	reduce(4)	
- x * y $	E + T	reduce(2)	ADD x y av[1]
- x * y $	E	shift	
x * y $	E -	shift	
* y $	E - x	reduce(7)	
* y $	E - F	reduce(4)	
* y $	E - T	shift	
y $	E - T *	shift	
$	E - T * y	reduce(8)	
$	E - T * F	reduce(5)	MUL x y av[2]
$	E - T	reduce(3)	SUB av[1] av[2] av[3]
$	E	accept	

Fig. 5.1:   Shift-reduce analysis and generation of quadruple code for the sentence
x + y - x * y.

Translation into Postfix Notation

In the following, grammar G_0 will be considered once more to exemplify semantic
actions generating postfix notation. To each production, the respective semantic
action A is added in the form (* A *); ADD, SUB, MUL, and DIV are obvious while
LOD is a load operation to push operands onto the stack. Then the production set
of G_0 is given as follows:

EXPR	→	TERM	(* T *)
EXPR	→	EXPR + TERM	(* E T ADD *)
EXPR	→	EXPR - TERM	(* E T SUB *)
TERM	→	FACTOR	(* F *)
TERM	→	TERM * FACTOR	(* T F MUL *)
TERM	→	TERM / FACTOR	(* T F DIV *)
FACTOR	→	x	(* LOD x *)
FACTOR	→	y	(* LOD y *)
FACTOR	→	(EXPR)	(* E *)

Using these semantic actions we can produce the postfix notation for any sentence of the language generated by G_0. Consider the following leftmost derivation of the sentence $x + y - x * y$ and the according translation, where subscripts are introduced on certain nonterminals to distinguish these nonterminals clearly where they occur multiply in a production:

EXPR	$\rightarrow$	EXPR - TERM (* E T SUB *)
	$\rightarrow$	EXPR + $TERM_1$ - $TERM_2$ (* E T_1 ADD T_2 SUB *)
	$\rightarrow$	$TERM_3$ + $TERM_1$ - $TERM_2$ (* T_3 T_1 ADD T_2 SUB *)
	$\rightarrow$	FACTOR + $TERM_1$ - $TERM_2$ (* F T_1 ADD T_2 SUB *)
	$\rightarrow$	x + $TERM_1$ - $TERM_2$ (* LOD x T_1 ADD T_2 SUB *)
	$\rightarrow$	x + FACTOR - TERM (* LOD x F ADD T SUB *)
	$\rightarrow$	x + y - TERM (* LOD x LOD y ADD T SUB *)
	$\rightarrow$	x + y - TERM * FACTOR (* LOD x LOD y ADD T F MUL SUB *)
	$\rightarrow$	x + y - $FACTOR_1$ * $FACTOR_2$ (* LOD x LOD y ADD F_1 F_2 MUL SUB *)
	$\rightarrow$	x + y - x * FACTOR (* LOD x LOD y ADD LOD x F_2 MUL SUB *)
	$\rightarrow$	x + y - x * y (* LOD x LOD y ADD LOD x LOD y MUL SUB *)

Thus, the translation of the sentence $x + y - x * y$ into postfix notation is

    LOD x LOD y ADD LOD x LOD y MUL SUB

which corresponds to the example given in the previous section.

This translation scheme can be used not only for arithmetic expressions but for all features of a programming language. To exemplify this, the translation of PL/0 while-statements and if-statements into postfix notation is shown. PL/0 while-statements are given in the following form:

WHILE CONDITION **DO** STATEMENT

The translation of conditional and repetitional statements results in the generation of jump instructions. Since the destination address is in general not known when the jump instruction is generated, it is necessary to complete this information later. This can be done either using a *second pass* in which all the open addresses are fixed, or by using an array which contains the generated code and which can be accessed directly by the stored index of the jump instruction to *fixup* a destination address as soon as it is known. (Obviously, the usage of a code array has the disadvantage that the compiler programmer has to determine the maximum code size in advance. Another alternative will be the usage of *symbolic labels*.) Then, the general structure of the code for while-statements is:

> *L1:*
>
> > *Instructions to evaluate CONDITION*
> > *JPC L2*
> > *Instructions to execute STATEMENT*
> > *JMP L1*
>
> *L2:*
>
> > *...*

where JPC and JMP are conditional and unconditional jump instructions, respectively. A rudimentary code fragment for the generation of postfix code for PL/0 while-statements is given in Figure 5.2.

While a repetitional statement needs two jump instructions, the if-statement as given in PL/0 needs only one jump instruction. PL/0 if-statements are given in the following form:

IF CONDITION **THEN** STATEMENT

Analogously to the general code structure given above for while-statements, we can introduce the general code structure for if-statements:

> > *Instructions to evaluate CONDITION*
> > *JPC L1*
> > *Instructions to execute STATEMENT*
>
> *L1:*
>
> > *...*

Finally, Figure 5.3 shows a code fragment for the generation of postfix code for PL/0 if-statements (again, we use a code array).

```
code : ARRAY [0..codemax] OF RECORD
                               oc     : opcode;
                               level  : CARDINAL;
                               adr    : CARDINAL;
                            END;
(* code contains the generated intermediate code *)
(* oc: operation code; level: declaration level *)
(* adr: displacement address *)
...
IF  symbol = whilesym  THEN
  fix1 := cindex; (* cindex: code index *)
  Get_Symbol;
  Condition (...);   (* analyzes conditional expressions *)
  fix2 := cindex;
  CGen (JPC,0,0); (* generates code for a conditional *)
                  (* jump, where the address is undefined *)
  IF  symbol = dosym  THEN
    Get_Symbol
  ELSE
    Error(...)
  END;
  Statement (...);   (* analyzes executable statements *)
  CGen (JMP, 0, fix1); (* generates code for an *)
                       (* unconditional jump, adr: fix1 *)
  code[fix2].adr := cindex;  (* fixup JPC-address *)
END;
```

Fig. 5.2: Translation of while-statements

```
IF  symbol = ifsym  THEN
  Get_Symbol;
  Condition;
  IF  symbol = thensym  THEN
    Get_Symbol
  ELSE  Error(...)  END;
  fix1 := cindex; (* store the fixup address *)
  CGen(JPC,0,0); (* generates code for a conditional *)
                  (* jump, where the address is undefined *)
  Statement;
  code[fix1].adr := cindex;  (* adjust jump address *)
END;
```

Fig. 5.3: Translation of if-statements

5.3   Type Checking

Type checking is the way of ensuring that identifiers which are somehow related are of compatible types. Two identifiers are related

- by forming the left and right side of an operator;

- by forming the left and right side of an assignment statement;

- by being actual and formal parameters.

Consistency checks which are carried out before the execution of a source program (i.e. by the compiler) are said to be *static checks*, while those checks performed during the execution of a source program are called *dynamic checks* (or *run-time checks*). Checking the syntax is an example for static checks, while *type checks* are an example of checks which often can be done statically, and which sometimes must be done dynamically.

For example, consider the following declaration

```
str :   ARRAY [0..80] OF CHAR;
i   :   INTEGER;
```

In general, it cannot be guaranteed statically that the condition $0 \le i \le 80$ is fulfilled when using `str[i]`, i.e. this check has to be done dynamically. However, it is possible, for example, to check statically whether the assignment

```
str[i] := ch;
```

is allowed, i.e. whether both sides of the assignment statement are of compatible types. In order to do this the symbol table has to be consulted.

In the following, a brief example on how to introduce rules which allow type checking of arithmetic expressions is given. EType, TTYpe, and FType represent the type of an expression, term, etc.; subscripts are used to distinguish among the multiple occurrence of nonterminals. A subset of grammar G_0 with the according rules is given (assuming PL/0 semantics) as follows:

$$E \quad \rightarrow \quad T \qquad\qquad (^* \ EType := TType \ ^*)$$

$$E_1 \quad \rightarrow \quad E_2 + T \qquad (^* \ E_1Type := \text{if } E_2Type = \text{integer and}$$
$$TType = \text{integer then integer}$$
$$\text{else error\_type; } ^*)$$

$$T \quad \rightarrow \quad F \qquad\qquad (^* \ TType := FType \ ^*)$$

$$T_1 \quad \rightarrow \quad T_2 \ ^* F \qquad (^* \ T_1Type := \text{if } T_2Type = \text{integer and}$$
$$FType = \text{integer then integer}$$
$$\text{else error\_type; } ^*)$$

$$F \quad \rightarrow \quad x \qquad\qquad (^* \ FType := lookup\_Type(x); \ ^*)$$

$$F \quad \rightarrow \quad y \qquad\qquad (^* \ FType := lookup\_Type(y); \ ^*)$$

$$F \quad \rightarrow \quad (\ E\ ) \qquad\quad (^* \ FType := EType; \ ^*)$$

A procedure lookup_Type(...) is used to determine the type of an identifier by checking the symbol table. For example, the type of an expression formed by applying the plus-operator to a subexpression and a term is integer, if the type of both subexpression and term is integer, otherwise it is an error type.

Now, the formulation of rules for (PASCAL-like) semantics which state, for example, that integer * real results in a real, is obvious and it can be seen how a type will be propagated. Thus, during the semantic analysis process it can be determined where type coercions are required and which operators should be selected (e.g. floating-point or integer multiplication).

It should be noticed that not every programming language allows a static type checking as shown above. In the programming language APL, for example, the current value of a variable determines the variable's type. This means that the type of a variable can change during the program execution and, thus, has to be checked at run-time.

5.4 Intermediate Code Generation for PL/0

In the following a rudimentary code segment is given which is an expansion of the recursive descent parser of Chapter 4.3. It has got the same structure as the recursive descent parser and shows when the semantic actions are executed to generate the intermediate code. The intermediate code is a postfix notation using the following instruction set:

LIT	load a number (literal) n onto the stack;
LOD	fetch variable onto the stack;
STO	store variables according to assignment statements;
CAL	procedure call;
INT	increment stack pointer for storage allocation;
JMP	unconditional jump;
JPC	conditional jump;
ADD	add two operands from stack;
SUB	subtract two operands from stack;
MUL	multiply two operands from stack;
DIV	divide two operands from stack;
NEG	negate top of stack;
OD	top of stack odd?
EQ	are the two topmost stack elements equal?
NE	are the two topmost stack elements not equal?
LE	is top of stack less or equal (top of stack - 1)?
GE	is top of stack greater or equal (top of stack - 1)?
LS	is top of stack less than (top of stack - 1)?
GT	is top of stack greater than (top of stack - 1)?

```
PROGRAM Compiler;

    ...    ...    ...
PROCEDURE Hash (vn: alfa): INTEGER;
BEGIN
    ...
END Hash;


PROCEDURE InsertST (vn: alfa; k: object);
BEGIN
    ...
END InsertST;
```

```
PROCEDURE LookupST (VAR p: Hash_SymTab; vn: alfa) : INTEGER;
BEGIN
...
END LookupST;

PROCEDURE CGen (o: opcode; l: INTEGER; a: INTEGER);
BEGIN
  IF cindex > codemax THEN  Error(...);  END;
  WITH code[cindex] DO
    oc := o;
    level := l;
    adr := a
  END;
  INC(cindex)
END CGen;

PROCEDURE Block (lev: INTEGER);

  PROCEDURE Constdeclaration;
  BEGIN
    ...
  END Constdeclaration;

  PROCEDURE Vardeclaration;
  BEGIN
    ...
  END Vardeclaration;

  PROCEDURE Expression;
  VAR  ADDorSUB: symbols;
    PROCEDURE Term;
    VAR  MULorDIV: symbols;
      PROCEDURE Factor;
      VAR  i: INTEGER;
      BEGIN    (*Factor*)
        CASE symbol OF
          ident :   i := LookupST(HElement,id);
                    IF  i = 0  THEN  Error(...)
                    ELSE
                      WITH  HElement  DO
```

```
                        CASE  kind  OF
                          constobj:  CGen(LIT,0,val);
                          | varobj:    CGen(LOD,lev-level,addr);
                          | procobj:   Error(…);
                        END
                      END
                    END;
                    Get_Symbol
        | number:  CGen(LIT,0,num);  Get_Symbol;
        | lparen:  Get_Symbol; Expression;
                   IF  symbol = rparen  THEN  Get_Symbol
                   ELSE  Error(…)  END
        ELSE       Error(…)
      END;
    END Factor;


    BEGIN (*Term*)
      Factor;
      WHILE  symbol IN [times, slash]  DO
        MULorDIV := symbol;  Get_Symbol;  Factor;
        IF  MULorDIV = times  THEN
          CGen(MUL,0,0)
        ELSE
          CGen(DIV,0,0)
        END;
      END
    END Term;


  BEGIN (*Expression*)
    IF  symbol IN [plus, minus]  THEN
      ADDorSUB := symbol;  Get_Symbol;  Term;
      IF  ADDorSUB = minus  THEN  CGen(NEG,0,0)  END;
    ELSE  Term  END;
    WHILE  symbol IN [plus,minus]  DO
      ADDorSUB := symbol;  Get_Symbol;  Term;
      IF  ADDorSUB = minus  THEN
        CGen(SUB,0,0)
      ELSE
        CGen(ADD,0,0)
      END
    END
  END Expression;
```

```
PROCEDURE Condition;
VAR  compop : symbols;
BEGIN
  IF  symbol = oddsym  THEN
    Get_Symbol;  Expression;  CGen(OD,0,0);
  ELSE
    Expression;
    IF  symbol IN [eql,neq,lss,leq,gtr,geq]  THEN
      compop := symbol;  Get_Symbol;  Expression;
      CASE  compop  OF
        eql :  CGen(EQ,0,0);
      | neq :  CGen(NE,0,0);
      | lss :  CGen(LS,0,0);
      | geq :  CGen(GE,0,0);
      | gtr :  CGen(GT,0,0);
      | leq :  CGen(LE,0,0);
      END
    ELSE  Error(…)  END;
  END
END Condition;


PROCEDURE Statement;
VAR  i, fix1, fix2: INTEGER;
BEGIN
  CASE  symbol  OF
    ident :  i := LookupST(HEelement,id);
             IF  i = 0  THEN  Error(…)
             ELSIF  HElement.kind <> varobj  THEN
               Error(…)  END;
             Get_Symbol;
             IF  symbol = becomes  THEN  Get_Symbol
               ELSE  Error(…)  END;
             Expression;
             WITH  HElement  DO
               CGen(STO,lev-level,addr)
             END;
  | callsym: Get_Symbol;
             IF  symbol = ident  THEN
               i := LookupST(HElement,id);
               IF  i = 0  THEN  Error(…)
               ELSE
```

```
              WITH  HElement  DO
                IF  kind = procobj  THEN
                  CGen(CAL,lev-level,addr)
                ELSE  Error(…)  END;
              END;
              Get_Symbol
            END
          ELSE Error(…) END;
| ifsym:    Get_Symbol;
            Condition;
            IF  symbol = thensym  THEN  Get_Symbol
              ELSE  Error(…)  END;
            fix1 := cindex;  CGen(JPC,0,0);
            Statement;
            code[fix1].adr := cindex;
| beginsym:Get_Symbol;
            Statement;
            WHILE  symbol = semicolon  DO
              Get_Symbol; Statement
            END;
            IF  symbol = endsym  THEN  Get_Symbol
              ELSE  Error(…)  END
| whilesym:fix1 := cindex;  Get_Symbol;
            Condition;
            fix2 := cindex;  CGen(JPC,0,0);
            IF  symbol = dosym  THEN  Get_Symbol
              ELSE  Error(…)  END;
            Statement;
            CGen(JPU,0,fix1);
            code[fix2].adr := cindex;
  END
END Statement;

BEGIN (*Block*)

  …   …   …

END Block;

BEGIN (*Compiler*)

  …  Block (0);  …

END Compiler.
```

6 How to Handle Errors

A compiler is a system which in most cases has to *deal with an incorrect input*. Especially during the first developing steps of a program, a compiler will probably be used to perform those features which should be provided by a good syntax directed editing system, i.e. to find out if variables are not declared before using or if brackets are missing and things like that. Therefore, error handling is an important part of a compiler and the compiler writer always has to keep this fact in mind when designing a compiler.

It must be noted that the case of errors should already be considered when designing a programming language. Such a consideration is given, for example, if each statement of the programming language starts with a different keyword (except the assignment statement, of course). However, it is essential

- that a compiler is able to *detect errors* in an input,

- that a compiler *recovers from the errors* without losing too much information,

- and most of all that a compiler *produces an error message* which allows the programmer easily to find and correct the (syntactically) incorrect elements of his program.

Error messages of the form

```
***    Error 111    ***
***    Error occurred    ***
***    Missing declaration    ***
***    Missing delimiter    ***
```

are of no use for the programmer and should not occur in a well designed and user friendly compiling environment. For example, the error message `Missing declaration` could be replaced by

        ***   Variable *Name* not declared   ***

or for the missing delimiter it can be specified which delimiter is expected. In addition to such informative error messages it is of course desirable that the compiler produces a listing containing the source code and indicating in that listing where errors have occurred.

However, before considering error handling in lexical and syntactical analysis, possible errors have to be characterized and classified (Section 6.1). This classification will show that not every kind of error can be detected by a compiler.

6.1   Error Classification

During a problem solving process various possibilities exist on how errors can arise which are then reflected in the source code of a program. Considering errors from a compiler's view they can be subdivided into two categories:

- *visible errors*, and
- *invisible errors*.

Invisible errors in a program are undetectable by the compiler, since they do not result from an incorrect usage of the programming language, but from wrong decisions during the specification process or wrong formulations of algorithms. For example, writing

        a := b + c;   instead of   a := b * c;

can be detected neither by the compiler nor by the run-time system. Such logical errors do not affect the validity of a program in terms of its syntactic correctness. They are subject of formal program verification techniques which are not considered here. For more details about program verification see [LOEC 87], for example.

Visible errors - in contrast to logical errors - are detectable by the compiler or at least by the run-time system. Such errors can be characterized as follows:

- *spelling mistakes*, and
- errors which occur because of *disregarding formal requirements* of the programming language.

They will occur because the programmer is not sufficiently careful when programming. Errors of the latter kind may also occur because the programmer does not fully understand the language in which he is programming, or because he usually writes his programs in another language and, therefore, uses constructs of this language (such problems might appear when using programming languages like PASCAL and MODULA-2 in parallel, for example).

Occurrence Classification

The visible or compiler detectable errors are usually subdivided into three classes depending on the compiler phase in which the errors are detected:

- *lexical errors*;
- *syntax errors*;
- *semantic errors.*

A lexical error, for example, can be caused by using an invalid character, i.e. a character which does not belong to the vocabulary of the programming language or by the attempt to recognize a constant which produces an overflow.

A syntax error is detected when the parser expects a symbol which does not match the currently scanned symbol. LL- and LR-parsers have the advantage that they are both able to detect syntax errors at the earliest possible opportunity, i.e. an error message will be generated as soon as a symbol is scanned which cannot follow the sequence of symbols scanned so far.

Semantic errors belong to the semantics of a programming language which are in general not described by the grammar. The most frequent semantic errors are probably missing declarations.

In addition to these three error classes there are errors which will be detected by the run-time system because the compiler supplemented the generated code with certain actions for these cases. Such a typical

- *run-time error*

occurs when an array index is not an element of the specified sub-range or by the attempt to divide by zero. In such cases, the error will be reported and program execution will be stopped.

Statistical Classification

Ripley and Druseikis report some interesting results of the statistical analysis of syntax errors in [RIPL 78]. They investigated which errors PASCAL programmers make and discussed the results in relation to recovery strategies. The main result of the study was that syntax errors are most often very simple and that, in general, only one error per sentence occurs. The following summary gives an overview of the results:

- At least 40 % of the programs compiled were syntactically or semantically incorrect.

- 80 % of the incorrect statements had only one error.

- 13 % of the incorrect statements had two errors, less than 3 % had 3 errors, and the rest had 4 or more errors per statement.

- For about 50 % of the missing-token errors the ":" was missing, while a missing "END" was with 10.5 % on rank two.

- In about 13 % of the wrong-token errors a "," was written instead of a ";", and in more than 9 % ":=" was written instead of "=".

The occurring errors can be classified into four categories:

- punctuation errors,

- operator and operand errors,

- keyword errors, and

- other types of errors.

The statistical distribution over these four categories is given in Figure 6.1.

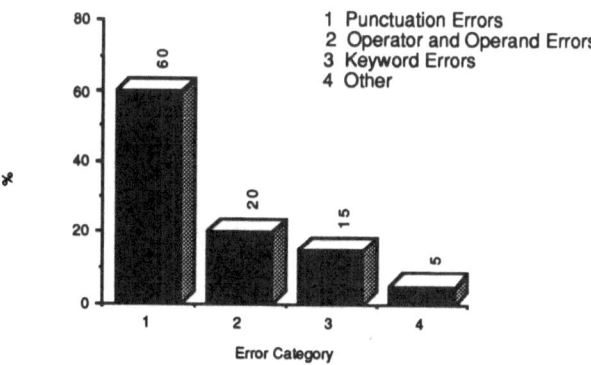

Fig. 6.1.   Statistical distribution over error categories according to [RIPL 78]

6.2   Effects of Errors

Detecting an error in a source code forces some reactions from the compiler. The behaviour of a compiler in case the source code contains an error can be many-sided:

- The compilation process *stops* at the occurrence of an error and the compiler should report the error.

- The compilation process *continues* when an error occurs and reports the error in a listing file.

- The compiler *does not recognize* the error and therefore gives no warning to the programmer.

The latter should never occur in a good compilation system, i.e. a compiler should be able to detect every visible error.

Stopping the compilation process when detecting the first error is the simplest way to fulfil the requirement that *a compilation must always terminate, no matter what the input looks like* [BRIN 85]. However, such a behaviour is also the worst in terms of a user friendly system, because a compilation may take several minutes. Therefore, the programmer expects a compilation system to find as many errors as possible, during a single compilation process.

Thus, in general, a compiler has to recover from an error to be able to check the source code for more errors. However, it must be noticed that any "repair" which the compiler carries out can just have the purpose of continuing to check for more errors, not to correct the source. Since there are no well-defined general rules formulated how to recover from an error, the recovery process must be based on hypotheses about errors. The lack of such rules is due to the fact that error recovery always depends on the individual language.

6.3   Error Handling in Lexical Analysis

Lexical errors are detected when the scanner attempts to recognize tokens in the source code. Typical lexical errors are:

- *illegal identifier names*: a name contains invalid characters;

- *invalid numbers*: a number contains either invalid characters (e.g. 2,13 instead of 2.13), is badly formed (e.g. 0.1.33), or is too large and, therefore, produces an overflow;

- *incorrect character strings*: a character string is too long (probably because of a missing closing quote);

- *spelling errors in reserved words*: missing, additional, misspelled, or mixed characters;

- *illegal labels*: a label is too long or contains invalid characters;

- *end of file*: an end of file in the middle of a token is reached.

Most of the lexical errors are careless mistakes which the programmer has overlooked. Recovery from lexical errors is in general relatively simple.

If a name, a number or a label contains an invalid character, the character is deleted and scanning is resumed at the next character, i.e. the scanner starts to recognize the next token. The effect is the generation of a syntax error which will be detected by the parser. This method can also be applied to badly formed numbers.

Character sequences like 12AB could occur when an operator is missing - the most improbable case - or when certain characters are misspelled. It is impossible for the scanner to decide whether such a sequence is an illegal identifier or an illegal number. In such cases the scanner can either skip the whole string or can try to break up the illegal sequences into shorter legal sequences. No matter what the decision is, a syntax error will be the consequence.

The detection of strings which are too long is not very complicated even when the closing quote is missing, since strings are normally not allowed to cross line boundaries. When a closing quote is missing the end-of-line character can be taken as the closing quote and scanning is resumed in the next line. This repair probably forces additional errors. In any case, the programmer must be informed by an error message.

Similar to the missing closing quote of a string is a missing closing comment symbol. Since comments are usually allowed to be multilined, a missing closing comment symbol cannot be detected until the scanner reaches the end of the file or finds a closing comment symbol which belongs probably to another comment (if nested comments are not allowed).

If it is known that the next token is supposed to be a reserved word, it is possible to correct a misspelled reserved word. This can be done either using error correction functions as they are well known in natural language systems, or simply applying some metric distance function between the input sequence and the set of reserved words.

Finally, the compilation process can simply be terminated, if an end-of-file is found within a token.

6.4   Error Handling in Syntax Analysis

A syntax error is detected by the parser when the scanner provides the next symbol which is incompatible with the current state of the parser. Typical syntax errors are for example:

- *missing brackets or parentheses*, e.g. x := y * (1 + z ;

- *missing operators or operands*, e.g. x := y (1 + z) ;

- *missing delimiters*, e.g. x := y + 1   IF a THEN y := z.

There are no generally valid error recovery strategies available and most of the known strategies are heuristic, because they are based on assumptions how errors might occur and what a programmer probably meant by a certain construct. Anyhow, a few strategies are widely accepted:

- *Panic recovery*: When detecting an error the parser skips all input symbols until a symbol of a predefined set of synchronizing symbols occurs. Such synchronizing symbols are the semi-colon, the end symbol or any keyword which can be the beginning of a new statement, for example. Panic recovery is very simple to implement, but it recognizes only one error per statement. This need not be a disadvantage, since it seems to be not very likely that multiple errors occur in one statement (see [RIPL 78], for example). The latter assumption is a typical example for the heuristic characteristic of the strategy.

- *Recovery by insertion, deletion, and replacement*: This is also a very easy to implement method and it works well in certain error cases. Let us take a PASCAL variable declaration as an example. Whenever a comma is followed by a colon instead of another variable name, this comma can be deleted. In the same way a missing semi-colon can be inserted, or a semi-colon in a parameter list can be replaced by a comma.

- *Recovery by grammar expansion*: According to [RIPL 78] 60 % of the errors in source programs are punctuation errors, e.g. writing a semi-colon instead of a comma or vice versa. One way to recover from such errors is to legalize them in certain cases by introducing so-called error productions into the grammar of the programming language. The expansion of a grammar by such productions does not mean that certain errors will remain undetected since actions can be inserted to report them.

Panic recovery is the strategy which will be found in most compilers, but the legalization of certain errors by defining an augmented grammar is also a widely used technique. Nevertheless, a grammar must be expanded carefully to ensure that the grammar's type and characteristics are not changed.

Syntax errors are detected when the parser expects a symbol which does not match the currently scanned symbol α. In LL-parsers syntax errors are recognized when α does not match the terminal on top of the stack, or when α together with the nonterminal on top of the stack indexes an empty position in the parse table. In LR-parsers syntax errors are recognized when indexing an empty position in the table, i.e. when no transition is specified for scanning α in the current state (cf. Chapter 4). However, if an augmented grammar with additional error productions is used, errors will not only be detected when indexing an empty position of the parse table.

6.5   Semantic Errors

Errors which can be detected by the parser are those errors which violate the rules of a context-free grammar. It was already mentioned that some characteristics of a programming language cannot be stated by context-free rules, since they are context-sensitive, e.g. the restriction that identifiers must be pre-declared. Thus, the main semantic errors are:

- *undefined identifiers*;

- *incompatible operators and operands*.

It is even more difficult to introduce formal methods for semantic error recovery than for syntactic error recovery, because semantic error recovery is often done *ad hoc*. Nevertheless, it can be required that a semantic error will at least be reported to the programmer, that it is just ignored and that therefore code generation will be suppressed.

However, most of the semantic errors can be detected by checking the symbol table. If an undefined identifier is detected, it is desirable to insert the identifier into the symbol table, assuming a type which is based on the context where it occurs or a universal type which allows the identifier to be an operand of any operator of the language. Doing this, we avoid that an error message is output each time the undefined variable is used. If an operand's type does not match the type requirements of an operator, it is also suitable to replace the operand by a dummy of universal type.

6.6 PL/0 Error Recovery

In the following, some of the above-mentioned methods for syntax error recovery will be exemplified by expanding program fragments of the *recursive descent parser* for PL/0 of Chapter 4.

Panic Recovery

The idea of recursive descent parsing is that a parsing problem is divided into sub-problems which are solved recursively. Now, the occurrence of an error in a sub-problem means that this error should not just be reported to the calling procedure. Rather, it must be guaranteed that the procedure for the sub-problem recovers from the error in a way that the calling procedure can continue the parse process, i.e. that it terminates regularly.

Thus, besides the generation of an error message, the input must be skipped until a synchronizing symbol is reached. This implies that each procedure of a recursive descent parser must know its valid follow symbols. To avoid uncontrolled skipping of symbols, the sets of follow symbols are augmented by sets of additional stop symbols indicating constructs which should not be skipped. The follow symbols and stop symbols together form the synchronizing symbols.

```
PROCEDURE Test(follow, stop: symset; n: INTEGER);
  (* follow, stop: synchronizing symbols  *)
  (* n:  just an error number             *)
VAR syncs : symset;
BEGIN
  IF NOT (symbol IN follow)  THEN
    Error(n);
    syncs := follow + stop;
    WHILE  NOT (symbol IN syncs)  DO  Get_Symbol  END
  END
END Test;
```

Fig. 6.2.   Procedure for checking and skipping symbols

```
PROCEDURE Expression (follow: symset);
VAR   ADDorSUB: symbols;
  PROCEDURE Term (follow: symset);
  VAR   MULorDIV: symbols;
    PROCEDURE Factor (follow: symset);
    VAR   i: INTEGER;
    BEGIN    (*Factor*)
      Test(factstart,follow,…);
      WHILE   symbol IN factstart   DO
        …
        Test(follow,[lparen],…)
      END
    END Factor;
    BEGIN (*Term*)
      Factor(follow + [times,slash]);
      WHILE   symbol IN [times, slash]   DO
        MULorDIV := symbol;  Get_Symbol;
        Factor(follow + [times,slash]);
        …
      END
    END Term;
  BEGIN (*Expression*)
    …
  END Expression;
```

Fig. 6.3.   Usage of the test procedure

This means for the implementation that each parsing procedure consists of a parameter specifying the set of valid follow symbols. The test for synchronizing symbols can be performed easily using the procedure shown in Figure 6.2. This procedure tests whether a follow symbol is legal. In case of an illegal symbol, an error message is generated and input symbols are skipped until a synchronizing symbol is reached. This test procedure will then be called at the end of each procedure to verify that the next symbol is a valid follow symbol, but it may also be used at the beginning of a parse procedure to verify whether the current input symbol is an admissible initial symbol. The usage of the test procedure is exemplified in Figure 6.3 for the parsing of arithmetic expressions (where factstart indicates admissible start symbols of Factor).

Grammar Expansion

As already mentioned, it is a well known fact that punctuation errors are very frequent. As an example, take constants in PL/0 which are separated by commas; a frequent error one could think of might be the usage of a semi-colon instead of a comma. Knowing such a fact, the syntactical structure of constant declarations can be changed in a way that both comma and semi-colon will be allowed, as shown in Figure 6.4.

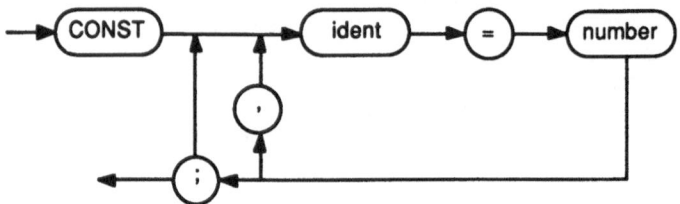

Fig. 6.4.   Modified syntax of constant declaration

```
IF  symbol = constsym  THEN
  Get_Symbol;
  REPEAT
    Constdeclaration;
    WHILE  symbol = comma  DO
      Get_Symbol; Constdeclaration
    END;
    IF  symbol = semicolon  THEN  Get_Symbol
    ELSE  Error(…)  END;
  UNTIL (symbol <> ident);
END;
```

Fig. 6.5.   Modified code for analyzing constant declarations

The modified constant declaration of Figure 6.4 legalizes the error described above. The syntax diagram of Figure 6.4 can then be translated into the program fragment of Figure 6.5 using the techniques introduced in Chapter 4.

The program fragment of Figure 6.5 allows the separation of constants by commas or semi-colons without producing an error message. In addition to this legalization it will be accepted that both the comma and the semi-colon can be omitted. In this case, however, an error message will be produced. It is obvious that in the same way the syntax of variable declarations can be expanded to allow variable separation by semi-colon or even by space (cf. Figure 6.6).

```
IF   symbol = varsym   THEN
  Get_Symbol;
  REPEAT
    Vardeclaration;
    WHILE   symbol = comma   DO
      Get_Symbol; Vardeclaration
    END;
    IF   symbol = semicolon   THEN   Get_Symbol
    ELSE   Error(...)   END;
  UNTIL (symbol <> ident);
END;
```

Fig. 6.6.   Modified code for analyzing variable declarations

```
IF   symbol = beginsym   THEN
  Get_Symbol;
  REPEAT
    statement(follow+[semicolon,endsym]);
    WHILE   symbol = semicolon   DO
      Get_Symbol;
      statement(follow+[semicolon,endsym]);
    END
  UNTIL   NOT (symbol IN statbegsys);
  IF   symbol = endsym   THEN
    Get_Symbol
  ELSE   Error(...)   END;
END;
```

Fig. 6.7.   Modified code for analyzing statements

Analogously, it can be allowed that the semi-colon between two statements can be omitted. This is shown in the program fragment in Figure 6.7, where statbegsys is the set of start symbols of statements.

7 Code Generation and Optimization

Finally, the compilation system reaches the phase of code generation. The input of the code generator is the intermediate code which was produced during syntactic or semantic analysis. The output of the code generator is a sequence of instructions which facilitates the execution of the source code by a specific hardware (see Figure 7.1).

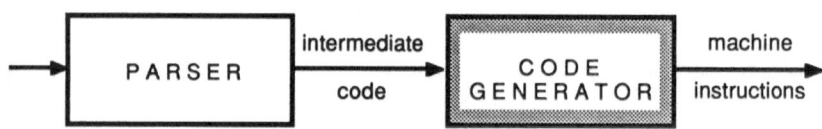

Fig. 7.1. Code generation

Thus, code generation depends not only on the chosen intermediate representation, but also on the target hardware and the instruction set of that hardware. However, code generation is probably the most important part of a compiler, since good code can be much faster in execution than badly generated code.

The generated code can be either

- *absolute code,* or

- *relocatable code.*

Absolute code means the generation of actual machine code with complete memory addresses, while relocatable code means the generation of code with address offsets. Thus, relocatable code can subsequently be linked with other object codes, e.g. library subroutines or any other separately compiled module.

Although it is difficult to formulate general algorithms for code generation (because of the machine dependent treatment of the topic) a few aspects which can be found in almost any code generator will be introduced in this Chapter. Before, however, it is essential to consider storage allocation techniques.

7.1 Storage Allocation

It was shown in the previous Chapters that the declaration of a name and the subsequent usage of this name result in symbol table manipulations. For code generation the information of the symbol table must be transformed into storage addresses. Thus, storage allocation in terms of code generation means the assignment of memory space for the storage of names as well as compiler defined auxiliary variables and additional information for procedures, such as the return address.

It must be distinguished between

- *static allocation*, and

- *dynamic allocation*.

During static allocation the storage space for names will be assigned during the compilation of the source program. This means that all names of the source code are bound to a fixed storage location and, therefore, exist during the whole lifetime of the program.

In contrast to this, dynamic allocation means that storage space for a name can be allocated and deallocated during the run-time of a program. This means that the names of a procedure are not bound to the same storage location each time the procedure is activated and especially that recursive procedures are possible. While FORTRAN is a typical example of a programming language with static storage allocation, block-oriented languages like PASCAL are typical examples for dynamic storage allocation.

Dynamic storage allocation allows different techniques:

- *stack allocation*, or

- *heap allocation*.

The first is used for recursive procedures, while heap allocation is useful for handling dynamic data structures, such as linked lists or trees.

7.1.1 Static Storage Allocation

The run-time address of each data object is known at compile-time when using static storage allocation. This implies that the compiler knows exactly

- the *number* of all objects, as well as

- the type and therefore the *size* of all objects.

Therefore, it is obvious that languages which permit static storage allocation do allow neither dynamic data structures, such as arrays with non-constant bounds or recursive structures which vary in size nor recursive procedure calls.

Figure 7.2 shows the memory organization of a hypothetical FORTRAN subroutine using static storage allocation.

The upper part of the storage contains the code for the subroutine itself, while the lower part contains the return address and probably other linkage information as well as the parameter list and possible compiler defined auxiliary variables.

```
SUBROUTINE  S  (P1, P2, … )
   …      …      …
RETURN
END
```

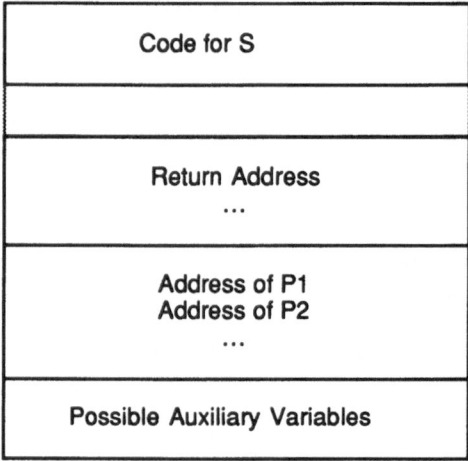

Fig. 7.2.   Storage organization of a FORTRAN subroutine

7.1.2 Dynamic Storage Allocation

Dynamic storage allocation is required when handling dynamic arrays or recursive data and program structures since the size of storage cannot be predicted at compile-time.

Stack Allocation

A stack organization of the memory is very suitable for dynamic storage allocation (run-time stack) and the handling of recursive procedures. The strategy then, is very simple: Each block of the program has its own data area. When invoking a block at run-time (e.g. calling a procedure), space for its data area (local variables as well as information about the procedure call/return mechanism) is allocated from the run-time stack, i.e. the data area is pushed onto the stack. When leaving the block, the space will be released, i.e. the data area is popped off the stack.

This strategy is exemplified by the program segment of Figure 7.3 containing recursively defined procedures. The contents of the run-time stack are traced in Figure 7.4.

```
PROGRAM  Dynsto;
VAR  x, y :  INTEGER;

   PROCEDURE P1;
   VAR  x, y :  INTEGER;

       PROCEDURE P2;
       VAR  k : INTEGER;

       BEGIN  ...  P2;  ...  END;

   BEGIN  ...  P2;  ...  END;

   PROCEDURE P3;
   VAR  i :  INTEGER

   BEGIN  ...  P1;  ...  END;

BEGIN  ...  P3;  ...  END.
```

Fig. 7.3. Program segment with recursive procedures

A possible sequence of procedure calls in the program segment of Figure 7.3 could be P3 P1 P2 P2, which is reflected in Figure 7.4.

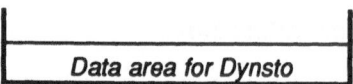

a)   Stack before calling P3

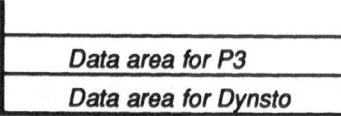

b)   Stack after calling P3

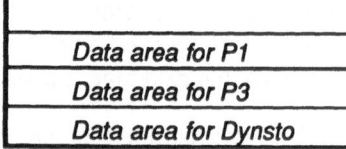

c)   Stack after calling P1

| Data area for P2 |
| Data area for P1 |
| Data area for P3 |
| Data area for Dynsto |

d)   Stack after calling P2

| Data area for P2 |
| Data area for P2 |
| Data area for P1 |
| Data area for P3 |
| Data area for Dynsto |

e)   Stack after calling P2 again

Fig. 7.4.   Stack organization: Trace of the run-time stack

In Figure 7.4 the data area of the main program (Dynsto) and the actually called procedures is shown for each state of the sequence P3 P1 P2 P2. The respective data areas are often referred to as *activation records*. Figure 7.4 e) shows clearly that each incarnation of a recursively defined procedure has its own data area or activation record, and that therefore in procedure P2 always the most recently defined variables - i.e. those variables, which belong to the current incarnation of P2 - will be accessed. It is clear that the activation record of a procedure does not only contain the local variables and/or parameters of the particular procedure but also information about the context, in which the procedure was called (i.e. the return address, for example). Thus, the data area of a procedure consists of

- parameters,

- local variables, and

- contextual information.

The contextual information itself consists of three addresses:

- the return address,

- the dynamic link, and

- the static link.

Clearly, the procedure's *return address* is that address to where the control must be transferred, when the procedure terminates.

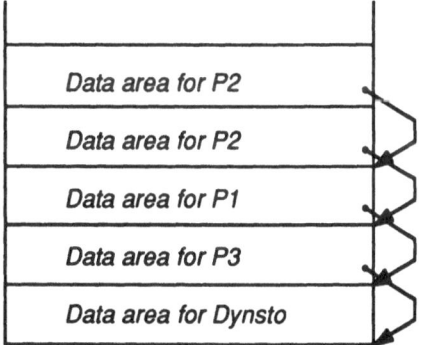

Fig. 7.5.   Dynamic chain belonging to Fig. 7.4 e)

Transfer of control is not the only thing which must be done, when terminating a procedure; there is also the stack, which has to be reorganized, i.e. the procedure's activation record must be released. The removal of an activation record is supported by the *dynamic link*, which is the base address of the previous data area within the stack. The chain of dynamic links is referred to as *dynamic chain*. It is called dynamic because it represents the dynamic structure in which procedures are activated. The dynamic chain of Figure 7.4 e) is shown in Figure 7.5.

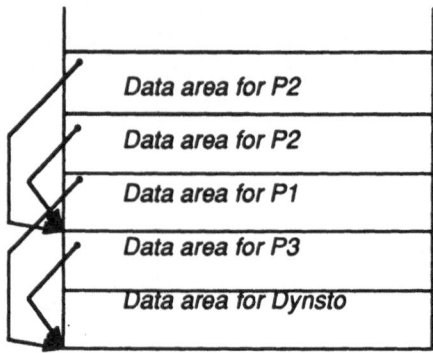

Fig. 7.6.   Static chain belonging to Fig. 7.4 e)

Since procedures should not only have access to their local variables, but also to other (global) variables of their context (i.e. all variables of the surrounding blocks), the currently accessible variables must be defined. This is usually done by using a *static link*, which is the base address of the data area forming the environment or context of the procedure, or - generally speaking - the block. The chain of static links is referred to as *static chain*. It is called static because it reflects the static nesting structure of blocks or procedures in the source code. Clearly, the static chain is in general different from the dynamic chain (especially when considering recursive procedures). The static chain of Figure 7.4 e) is shown in Figure 7.6.

A static link of a given block references the activation record or data area of the statically surrounding block (e.g. P2 is surrounded by P1 in the program segment of Figure 7.3) and, therefore, allows the access to nonlocal variables. In case of such an access to nonlocal variables, the compiler generates code in order to follow an appropriate number of static links (obviously, the compiler can generate such a code, since the nesting structure of a source code is static and known at compile-time). Then, when the correct data area has been found, the desired variable can be accessed via an offset from the corresponding base address. This can be very time consuming when the nesting level is accordingly deep.

An alternative for handling the access to nonlocal variables will be given by introducing a so-called *display* whenever storage is allocated from the stack to a data area. A display is simply a vector or table of pointers to those activation records containing accessible variables. Thus, a display is just another representation of the static chain. A display will be initialized by copying the calling block's display to the display of the called block; additional, the base address of the calling block will be entered to the new display. A nonlocal variable is accessed via an offset from the corresponding base address which is found in the display. The display can be a part of a block's data area, i.e. it is stored on the stack. There are other possibilities to keep the display. If there is an acceptable number of registers available, then these registers might be used to maintain the display. It must be mentioned, however, that in this case the maximum nesting depth of the source code will be limited according to the number of available registers. Other possibilities to maintain displays are discussed in [FISC 88], for example. Applying displays to the data areas shown in Figure 7.4 e) results in Figure 7.7.

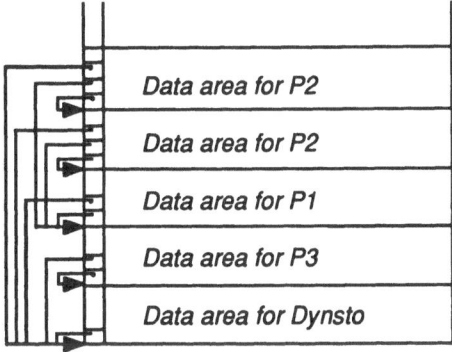

Fig. 7.7.   Displays belonging to Fig. 7.4 e)

Heap Allocation

The handling of dynamic data structures is usually done by allocating the required storage from the heap, a storage pool from which space can be allocated and freed at any time and in any order during the execution of a program. Usually, space is allocated on the stack for a pointer, which points to a storage block in the heap containing the data and a descriptor indicating the size of the data object. The situation is illustrated in Figure 7.8.

In different programming languages certain ways to require heap allocation for dynamic data structures exist. In PASCAL or MODULA-2, for example, the *new* and *dispose* procedures are available for the programmer to explicitly allocate and deallocate storage during run-time. In other languages - like SNOBOL or LISP - storage allocation and deallocation might be implicit, e.g. the usage of variable length character strings in SNOBOL.

In general, heap allocation is not very complicated, but the availability of a heap management is required. Since it is possible to deallocate storage in any order, strategies to manage and to combine the free storage blocks are necessary. Free storage blocks are usually linked together in a free-list (cf. Figure 7.8).

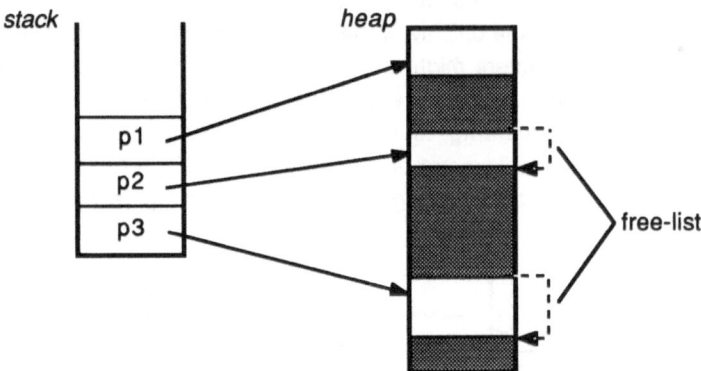

Fig. 7.8. Heap allocation

With the *dispose* procedure in PASCAL or MODULA-2 storage can be explicitly deallocated, and in such languages it is normally the user's responsibility to free storage. Other languages require implicit deallocation or garbage collection (i.e. the process to find un-used space in the heap and to return it to the free-list). There are different strategies available for implicit deallocation. The simplest way to deallocate implicitly is to use *reference counts*, i.e. a counter indicating the number of pointers to a given data object. A zero counter causes the storage space of the data object to be inserted into the free-list.

7.2 Parameter Passing

As was mentioned in the previous section the data area of a procedure consists not only of local variables and contextual information but also of parameters. So the question how to pass parameters from a surrounding block to an inner block is important. Various techniques of parameter passing are known; the most important ones (call by value, call by reference, call by value-result, and call by name) are explained in the following.

Call by Value

Call by value means that the value of the actual parameter is copied into the storage space of the formal parameter, when calling the procedure. Thus, formal parameters can be treated like local variables, i.e. storage allocation and access is the same as for local variables. Code must be generated to perform the copy operation, which can result in a considerable overhead when passing large data structures by value. Clearly, in this case data can be passed into a procedure, but not out of the procedure.

Call by Reference

Call by reference means that the address of the actual parameter is passed to the procedure, instead of the value. Thus, the location of the formal parameter contains just the address where to find and/or to change the data, i.e. each parameter access requires instructions for indirect addressing. Intensive access to reference parameters in a procedure can therefore cause an overhead. It is clear that in this case data can be passed into and out of a procedure.

Call by Value-result

Call by value-result lies between call by reference and call by value. The actual parameter is copied to the formal parameter, when entering the procedure, and it is copied back when terminating the procedure. Thus, parameters can be accessed like local variables. Since there are two copy operations, the disadvantage of the call by value technique is doubled, but the disadvantage of the call by reference technique does not occur. Obviously, this technique should only be applied when passing simple type variables.

Call by Name

Call by name means that the actual parameter textually substitutes the formal parameter, whenever it occurs. The traditional technique of implementation is to treat the procedure as a macro, i.e. the compiler replaces each call of the procedure by the procedure's body, formal parameters are textually substituted by the actual parameters and local names are kept distinct from names in the calling block.

7.3   Variable Addressing

Addressing of variables is in general not very complicated. However, it will be discussed in this Chapter.

Simple Variables

Addressing simple variables (e.g. an integer variable) works on a very elementary principle. Memory space (starting at a particular address) has to be provided for the storage of the variables. A variable declaration, then, causes the allocation of space in this data area, which is usually done using a pointer to the next free space. Addressing variables is now very simple, using the data area's base address and an appropriate offset. This general technique of using a base address and an offset is the same for both non-block-structured languages and block-structured languages. In the latter case, of course, not only one data area exists, but several dynamically created areas (cf. Section 7.1).

Arrays

The handling of fixed-size arrays (i.e. arrays where the upper and lower bounds, and hence the size of the array are known at compile-time) is not very difficult. The general technique of variable addressing as introduced above can also be applied to fixed-size arrays as demonstrated below. The access to an element a[i] of a one-dimensional array a[l1..u1] is given by the address

$$base_a + (i - l1) * size ,$$

where $base_a$ denotes the address of the first element of the array (i.e. a[l1]) in the data area, l1 (u1) denotes the lower (upper) bound of the array, and size is the size of storage (counted in words or bytes), which must be allocated to store a single element of the array (depending on the array's type, of course).

Multidimensional arrays must be mapped to a linear structure in order to be stored. This can be done in

- *row-major* form, or

- *column-major* form.

Row-major form means that the array elements are stored with the rightmost index varying the most rapidly, while in column-major form the array elements are stored with the leftmost index varying the most rapidly. Figure 7.9 shows a two-dimensional array a[3..4, 2..5] stored in row-major form.

a [3, 2]
a [3, 3]
a [3, 4]
a [3, 5]
a [4, 2]
a [4, 3]
a [4, 4]
a [4, 5]

Fig. 7.9.   Row-major form for storing a two-dimensional array

The address of an element a[i, j] of a two-dimensional array a[l1..u1, l2..u2] is then given for row-major forms as

$$base_a + ((i - l1) * (u2 - l2 + 1) + (j - l2)) * size$$

and for column-major forms as

$$base_a + ((j - l2) * (u1 - l1 + 1) + (i - l1)) * size.$$

In case both lower bounds are 0, these address formulas can be simplified to

$$base_a + (i * (u2 + 1) + j) * size$$

and

$$base_a + (j * (u1 + 1) + i) * size,$$

respectively.

Using these formulas, we can determine the address of the array element a [4, 4] (cf. Figure 7.9) as

$$
\begin{aligned}
adr\ (a[4,4]) &= base_a + ((4 - 3) * (5 - 2 + 1) + (4 - 2)) * size \\
&= base_a + 6 * size
\end{aligned}
$$

for row-major form, and

$$
\begin{aligned}
adr\ (a[4,4]) &= base_a + ((4 - 2) * (4 - 3 + 1) + (4 - 3)) * size \\
&= base_a + 5 * size
\end{aligned}
$$

for column-major form.

The handling of dynamic arrays (i.e. arrays whose upper and/or lower bounds, and hence whose size are only known at run-time) is a bit more complicated. The problem can be solved by generating an array descriptor at compile-time, which will be initialized at run-time. The descriptor reserves space to hold the information about the array (e.g. number of dimension, upper and lower bounds). Obviously, dynamic storage allocation techniques as introduced in Section 7.1.2 are needed to maintain dynamic arrays. The addressing of array elements is the same as for fixed-size arrays, but the upper and lower bounds must be taken from the descriptor.

Records

Addressing records is as basic as addressing arrays. The access to an entire record variable is obviously simple, e.g. an assignment of a record variable r1 to another r2 will be carried out by copying the memory space belonging to r1 into the area of r2. Clearly, individual record elements can be accessed using the base address of the record and an appropriate offset. Using records to define dynamic data structures, e.g. linked lists, will require storage allocation techniques as explained in Section 7.1.2.

7.4   Code Generation

The function of a code generator is basically the translation of the output from the syntactic and semantic analysis (i.e. the intermediate code) into an equivalent sequence of instructions which can be executed on the target machine. Two essential requirements exist for the output of a code generator:

- the produced code *must be correct*, and

- the code *should be optimal.*

The first requirement is clearly a necessity, while the second requirement cannot be reached completely (in general). Since the generation of optimal code is an NP-complete problem, it is possible to generate high quality code, but not necessarily optimal code.

When generating machine code on the basis of an intermediary code it can be assumed that all necessary semantic checks have been carried out. That means that type checking and most of all type conversion has already taken place and that, therefore, the code generator need not take care of all the semantic rules of the programming language. However, the conclusion can by no means be that code generation is an easy process. In general, two basic decisions must take place when generating code.

- *Allocating Registers*: Since processors and language implementations often require that specific registers (or even/odd register-pairs) must be used for certain purposes, register allocation is a non-trivial task. Some machines, for example, separate general-purpose registers from index registers, and others may require the operands for certain instructions in even/odd register-pairs.

- *Selecting Instructions*: It is often possible to carry out a given computation in different ways. Choosing the best (i.e. 'optimal') sequence of instructions usually requires contextual knowledge which makes this decision non-trivial. A simple example is choosing an increment instruction (if available) instead of a sequence of MOV and ADD instructions, when incrementing a variable by one.

In addition to these two basic decisions which are common to nearly all code generators, a few other important things must be considered when generating code for a target hardware. Among them are the selection of the addressing mode as well as fixing the order of evaluation. The instruction set of a target machine, for instance, might only allow a subset of all possible addressing modes like the ADD instruction of some microprocessors, which does not allow memory-to-memory addition (i.e. either the source or the destination of this instruction must be a data register). Thus, the selected addressing mode may limit the available instructions in a certain case.

In the following, a very simple code generation (CG-) algorithm is introduced allowing the conversion of quadruples into machine code. This algorithm is based on basic blocks, register and address descriptors.

Basic Blocks

A *basic block* is a linear sequence of quadruples (or any other form of statements of an intermediary representation) containing no branches or halts except at the very end of the block. All statements of a basic block are executed in sequence, starting only on top of the block. Two basic blocks can be linked together by conditional or unconditional branch instructions. A source program can be represented by a linked chain of basic blocks.

1.	ADD	x	y	av1
2.	MUL	x	y	av2
3.	SUB	av1	av2	av3
4.	STO	av3		z

Fig. 7.10. A basic block

Figure 7.10 shows a sequence of quadruples which is an example for a basic block according to the source code statement z := x + y - x*y (cf. Chapter 5).

Register Descriptor

The information which registers hold the values of which variables (and by that the information which registers are free) at a certain time, is kept in a *register descriptor*. Using such a descriptor, it is possible to indicate that a register can hold the value of more than one variable at a time (e.g. as a result of simple copy instructions). The register descriptor is used when allocating a new register.

Address Descriptor

In contrast to the register descriptor, the *address descriptor* shows the locations (stack, register and/or memory) in which the current value of the variables can be found. The information is used when access to a variable is required, and it is usually a part of the symbol table.

The CG-Algorithm

Let us assume that the code generator produces a kind of assembler code in the two address form

    · *operation   source, destination.*

For example,

    SUB *source, destination*

means *destination := destination - source.*

Further, let us assume that we have a target machine with instructions where the destination operand in all arithmetic and logical instructions must be a register, similar to many of the popular microprocessors.

The code generation (CG-) algorithm is given in form of a procedure with two parameters, a basic block and the length of the basic block (cf. Figure 7.11). To simplify matters, the basic block parameter is assumed to be an array of records representing the intermediary quadruple representation:

```
Quad          =    RECORD
                        Op   :  Operator;
                        Arg1 :  Name;
                        Arg2 :  Name;
                        Res  :  Name;
                   END;

BasicBlock    =    ARRAY [1..max] OF Quad;
```

```
PROCEDURE CG (BB: BasicBlock; BBlength: INTEGER);
VAR
      i        :   INTEGER;
      res, loc :   Location;
                  (* register or memory location *)

BEGIN

  FOR  i := 1  TO  BBlength  DO

    LocateResult (BB[i], res);
    FindArg (BB[i].Arg1, loc);
    IF  loc <> res  THEN
      MCode ('MOVE', loc, res);
    END;

    FindArg (BB[i].Arg2, loc);
    MCode (BB[i].Op, loc, res);

    AddressUpdate (BB[i].Res, res);
    IF  res IN Registers  THEN
      RegisterUpdate (BB[i].Res, res);
    END

  END;

  MemoryUpdate;

END (* CG *);
```

Fig. 7.11. The CG-algorithm

The different procedures in the algorithm of Figure 7.11 are described in the following.

FindArg (arg, loc): determines the current location of *arg*, performing a preference relation $<_\lambda$ for every location of *arg*. The preference mem $<_\lambda$ reg signifies that a register location is more useful than a memory location.

LocateResult (quad, res): determines the location where the result of a quadruple (*quad.Res*) should be placed, taking into consideration the location of *quad.Arg1* and performing the preference relation $<_\lambda$ together with certain conditions, e.g. that the register location of *quad.Arg1* is not permitted to hold the value of other variables, too. If no free register is available, an occupied register must be stored on memory to return a free register in *res*. The decision which register to free can be based preferably on Belady's famous and optimal swapping algorithm [BELA 66], i.e. that register will be freed whose next access is furthest in the future.

MCode (op, source, dest): outputs machine instructions according to the actual parameters. It is assumed that for each intermediary operator an equivalent machine instruction (or a set of instructions) exists.

AddressUpdate (x, p): updates the address descriptor of *x* (in the symbol table), indicating that *x* can be found in location *p*.

RegisterUpdate (x, r): updates the register descriptor of *r*, indicating that *r* contains the value of *x*.

MemoryUpdate: updates the memory locations of those variables whose values have changed in registers and which are not already stored on memory.

Applying the algorithm of Figure 7.11 to the basic block of Figure 7.10 will result in the sequence of instructions shown in Figure 7.12.

1.	MOVE	x,	R0
2.	ADD	y,	R0
3.	MOVE	x,	R1
4.	MUL	y,	R1
5.	MOVE	R0,	R2
6.	SUB	R1,	R2
7.	MOVE	R2,	z

Fig. 7.12. Machine instructions according to the example of Fig. 7.10

Obviously, the sequence of instructions in Figure 7.12 is not optimal. Copying the contents of register R0 into register R2, for example, is unnecessary because the variable av1 is only used in the third quadruple of Figure 7.10. Therefore, instruction 5 can be omitted and instruction 6 can be changed to SUB R1, R0. However, this can only be done by performing a data-flow analysis (as described in [ALLE 76] or [AHOS 86], for example). More about code optimization is shown in the following Section 7.5.

The CG-algorithm shown requires quadruples as an input. If the intermediate code is an *abstract syntax tree*, we are interested in a tree-traversing algorithm to produce the desired target code. Such an algorithm could be based on general tree-traversing algorithms and would probably be simpler in its implementation. The representation of basic blocks by *directed acyclic graphs* (DAG's) is another useful method which is explained in more detail in [AHOS 86].

7.5   Code Optimization

As mentioned above, the generation of optimal code is an NP-complete problem and therefore, the so-called optimizing compilers do in general *not* produce an optimal code. When talking about optimization techniques, it must be noticed that optimization normally results in an *increased compile-time*. Therefore, the user often has the possibility to switch off the optimization part of the code generator during program development or debugging phase.

Many optimization techniques and optimizing compilers are described in literature. Code can be optimized in terms of

- *reducing* a program's *size*, or

- *increasing* a program's execution *speed*.

Since highly packed memory chips are now available at reasonable prices, reducing a program's size becomes less important, while optimizing run-time speed is still of vital interest. The term *optimization*, however, should not be misunderstood. Because of the NP-completeness of code generation, optimization can only mean the generation of better or improved code, but it does not mean the generation of the best possible code, in general.

Optimization techniques are based on extensive analysis of program structure and data flow. When optimizing, a program is usually subdivided into optimization regions, and the techniques used can be categorized as machine-independent and machine-dependent. Machine-independent optimization techniques need not consider knowledge of the hardware structure or instruction set of the target machine and are in this sense general (e.g. constant folding, as described later). In contrast, machine-dependent techniques need to know about hardware and the instruction set, since they affect things like register allocation or instruction selection.

Among the various optimization techniques the following ones are considered in this Section in more detail:

- constant folding;

- strength and frequency reduction;

- loop optimization;

- code elimination;

- rearrangements;

- peephole optimization.

Constant Folding

When different constants occur in an arithmetic expression, it may be possible to combine (*fold*) them into a single constant. For example, an assignment statement of the form

```
i := up - low + 5 ,
```

where `up` and `low` are the constants `up = 10` and `low = 1`, can be simplified to

```
i := 14 .
```

This calculation can be done at compile-time. It has the effect that the generated code needs less memory (because only one instead of three constants must be stored), and that the run-time speed of the program is increased (because the add and subtract operations are not performed at run-time).

Constant folding need not only concern a single statement, but can be applied to pairs of statements, too. Of course, this requires that a data flow analysis has taken place. Let us take as an example the sequence of assignments

```
i := 10;
k := i * 4;
```

which can be simplified to

```
i := 10;
k := 40;
```

if there is no other code between these two statements, changing `i`. Once more the code will need less memory and the execution time will be decreased.

Strength and Frequency Reduction

While *strength reduction* is the process by which an expensive (in terms of execution time) operation is replaced by a cheaper one, *frequency reduction* is the process by which certain computations are moved from one location to another location with the effect that these computations will be executed less frequently.

Typical optimizations using strength reduction are:

- Replacing an exponentiation operation by a faster multiplication operation, for example y ** 2 can be replaced by y * y.

- Replacing a multiplication operation within a loop by a faster addition operation, for example

```
FOR  i := 1  TO  10000  DO  h[i] := i * 2  END;
```

can be replaced by

```
FOR  i := 1  TO  10000  DO  h[i] := i + i  END;
```

Such a reduction is always possible for multiplications between the loop counter and a variable which does not change within the loop.

- Replacing power of two multiplication operations (i.e. x * 2, x * 4, x * 8, etc.) by arithmetic shift operations.

Frequency reduction is also known as *code motion*. If a loop contains computations which result in the same value each time the loop is executed, then such computations can be moved out of the loop (by introducing temporary variables, in certain circumstances). For example,

```
i := 0;
REPEAT
    x := x + h[i + j - k];   i := i + 3;
UNTIL (i > max - 3);
```

can be replaced by

```
t1 := j - k;
t2 := max - 3;
i := 0;
REPEAT
    x := x + h[i + t1];   i := i + 3;
UNTIL (i > t2);
```

Thus, more temporary storage is used to get a probably very strong increase of execution speed. Another example of code motion is given in the following discussion of loop optimization.

Loop Optimization

Loop optimization is probably that entity which produces the best results in terms of a program's execution time. Consider the following FOR-statement

```
FOR  i := 1  TO  10000  DO  h[i] := i + x * y  END;
```

Since x and y do not change within that loop, ten thousand multiplications can be replaced by a single multiplication, when moving the multiplication outside the loop. Obviously, execution speed is then increased. Thus, it is clear how the application of strength and frequency reduction techniques can be used for loop optimization.

Other optimization techniques for loops can be described as *optimization by combining* and *optimization by unrolling*. A sequence of loop statements, such as

```
FOR  i := 1  TO  10000  DO  h[i] := 1  END;
FOR  j := 1  TO  10000  DO  s[j] := j  END;
```

can be combined into a single loop, if they operate over the same range:

```
FOR  i := 1  TO  10000  DO  h[i] := 1;  s[i] := i  END;
```

If the body of a loop is very small and the number of times this body is executed is also low and known at compile-time, such as

```
FOR  i := 1  TO  5  DO  h[i] := 1  END;
```

it is possible to avoid the control code of that loop by replacing the loop by

```
h[1] := 1; h[2] := 1; h[3] := 1; h[4] := 1; h[5] := 1;
```

which is an equivalent sequential code.

Code Elimination

A further optimization technique is based on the *elimination of redundant code* and *common subexpressions*. A code is redundant, if it can never be reached, as for example in

```
b := FALSE;
IF  a AND b  THEN  ...  END;
```

or if an expression contains superfluous elements, as shown above: a AND b is always FALSE, whenever one of the operands is definitely FALSE. Redundant elements in arithmetic expressions are addition of 0, or multiplication by 1 (multiplication by 0 can be replaced by a simple CLR instruction). Such redundant elements will probably not be written by a programmer, but can be the result of the above introduced constant folding optimization.

Common subexpressions can be given explicitly by the programmer, such as

```
x := a / (j * k) - b / (j * k);
```

where j * k is the common subexpression, which can be eliminated by

```
t := j * k;    x := a / t - b / t;
```

However, common subexpressions can also be given implicitly, when indexing arrays which may involve multiplication and/or addition operations.

Rearrangements

In accordance with distributivity and associativity rules certain *rearrangements* in arithmetic or logical expressions can be made, resulting in reduced temporary storage and/or increased execution speed. Assuming a single accumulator machine, the expression

```
z := x + y + x * y;
```

for example, results in the following sequence of instructions

```
1.   MOVE     x    ACC
2.   ADD      y    ACC
3.   MOVE     ACC  R
4.   MOVE     x    ACC
5.   MUL      y    ACC
6.   ADD      R    ACC
7.   MOVE     ACC  z
```

When rearranging the expression, i.e.

```
z := x * y + x + y;
```

the instructions three and four are not necessary:

```
1.   MOVE     x    ACC
2.   MUL      y    ACC
3.   ADD      x    ACC
4.   ADD      y    ACC
5.   MOVE     ACC  z
```

Rearrangements in expressions using commutativity rules, such as x + y = y + x, are obvious and can result in simpler expressions.

Peephole Optimization

The idea of the peephole technique is to perform optimization by examining groups of instructions (the *peephole*). This technique can be machine-dependent, if the optimization is based on the instruction set of the target machine (see examples below). The technique can, however, also be machine-independent, if, for instance, the optimization is based on the intermediate code. Peephole optimization on intermediate code is discussed in [TANE 82] or [MCKE 89], for example.

Considering a group of instructions, an optimization can be accomplished in various ways.

- Replacing expensive instructions by cheaper instructions, for example

        MOVE   #0   R0

    can be replaced by a simple clear instruction which executes faster:

        CLR   R0

    Since most modern processors support an increment instruction,

        ADD   #1   R0

    can be replaced by

        INC   R0

    Similar to this is the usage of shift operations instead of multiplication operations, or the use of algebraic simplifications.

- Reducing redundant data transformations as they often occur in consecutive statements, e.g.

        MOVE   R0   x
        MOVE   x   R0

- Replacing chains of branch instructions by a single branch instruction, i.e. if control is transferred to another branch instruction, the address can be replaced by the final destination address.

Since optimizations can cause further optimizations or code improvements, the peephole optimization process needs repeated passes over the code to produce the best code improvement.

8 Impacts of Modern Hardware Developments

The preceding Chapters have shown that in compilers we can find many algorithms and concepts which are more or less independent of the target hardware. We have also seen, though, that code generation and optimization is a non-trivial process depending strongly on the target hardware, i.e. on the instruction set of the target hardware and the available possibilities. Therefore, we want to conclude this book by a few remarks on the influences of hardware development on language and compiler design.

8.1 Computer Architectures vs. Programming Languages

Considering the evolutionary process of computer architectures and programming languages we will find that the *von Neumann architecture* had a great influence on customary programming languages. In the von Neumann architecture a control unit, a processing unit, and input/output units are built around a memory unit containing data and instructions (cf. Figure 8.1).

Traditional von Neumann computers execute instructions one after another. This is reflected in the sequential structure of conventional programming languages like FORTRAN, ALGOL, PASCAL etc. Further, the memory locations of a von Neumann computer are represented in such languages by variables, the memory's modification is reflected by assignments to variables, and the control and test instructions of a von Neumann computer have their equivalence in the control statements of these programming languages. Thus, we understand the influence of the von Neumann architecture on the basic structures of our conventional programming languages and we can understand why Backus did not differentiate among conventional high level languages, but named all these languages *von Neumann languages* [BACK 78].

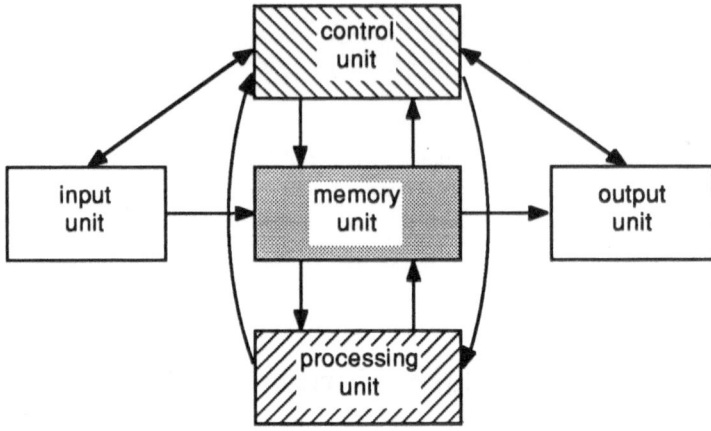

Fig. 8.1.   The von Neumann architecture

However, new trends in computer architecture exemplify that hardware can be designed corresponding to specific high level programming languages (e.g. functional languages) and, thus, directly support certain language constructs. We talk about *high level language architectures*. The probably most popular approaches towards this are the LISP machines whose hardware directly supports all the costly list operations. Other approaches to designing a hardware appropriate to the requirements of a specific programming language can not only be found for FORTH, PASCAL or PROLOG (see for example [YAMA 81] or [MILU 86]), but also for specific parts of programming languages, as was exemplified by a high accuracy arithmetic co-processor for PASCAL-SC (cf. [TEUF 84] or [TEUF 86]).

8.2   Instruction Sets and Microcode

In contrast to the arguments of the previous Section, the opinion that processor design is triggered by the requirements of high level programming languages and their compilers (or more or less the compiler writers) is held by some researchers. It is right that hardware designers have increased the mightiness of the instruction sets of new processors (up to the development of *reduced instruction set computer* (RISC) architectures), but it must be noticed that the programming languages are still von Neumann languages. Figure 8.2 schematically shows the changes of complexity of the processors' instruction sets over the last three decades.

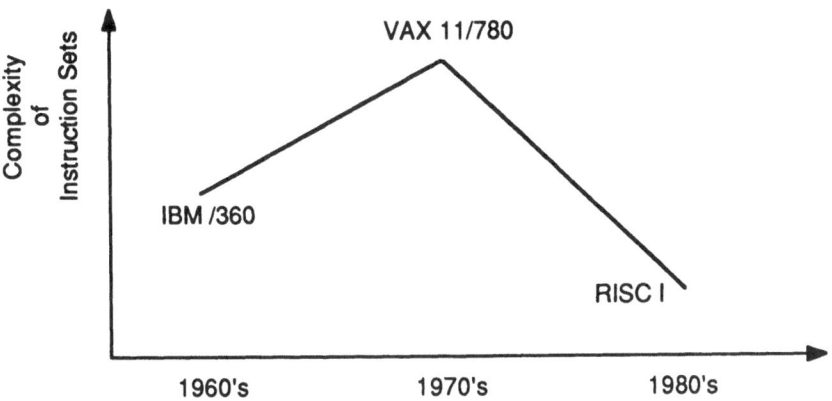

Fig. 8.2.   Complexity of instruction sets

The idea of *complex instruction set computers* (CISC) was to simplify compiler writing by providing richer instruction sets and, by this, to close the semantic gap between hardware and high level programming languages. The compiler writer was supposed to be supported by instruction sets that are more complex, but writing reliable compilers was by no means easier because of the complexity of the instruction set.

The instruction sets of CISC processors contain instructions which are close to specific programming language constructs (but it has to be noticed that they are designed for any conventional programming language and, therefore, need not be optimal for a certain language). Examples are:

- Decrement and branch (or increment and branch) instructions for the support of repetition statements.

- Multi-way jump instructions for the support of case-statements.

- Procedure call instructions for the support of procedure calls.

- Range checking instructions support the generation of code for subrange testing.

- String instructions support string handling.

Another step in the evolution of processors was the replacement (or at least partial replacement) of the fixed instruction set of a processor by microprogrammable instruction sets. That means that the instruction set of a microprogrammable processor is not fixed by the hardware, but can be programmed on a very low level.

The term microprogramming traces back to Wilkes who designed the control logic for the EDSAC II in the early fifties [WILK 51]. The basic ideas of microprogramming are shown in Figure 8.3.

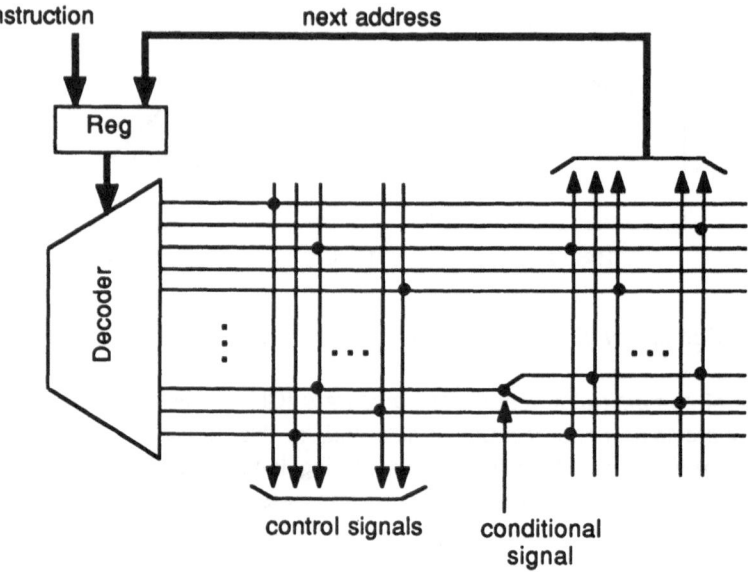

Fig 8.3.   Microprogrammed control unit

The heart of the system is a matrix partially filled with diodes. At each machine cycle one row of the matrix is activated through which control signals as well as signals to determine the next microcode address are generated. Thus, each row of the matrix corresponds to one microinstruction; the layout of the matrix determines the control logic. The advantage of such a structure is the highly regular structure which is usually held in a PROM.

The advantage of microprogrammable processors from the compiler writer's point of view is that the needs of a specific programming language can be considered by a carefully designed microinstruction set. There are also disadvantages, however, because microprogramming means programming on a very low level and is very troublesome. The generation of microcode allows no inefficiencies, since they directly cause an increase in execution time (which is different to slight inefficiencies in a high level language code).

8.3   RISC Architectures

Reduced instruction set computer architecture is one trend in the computer design of the eighties which was already initiated in the mid seventies when researchers began to think about the improvement of computer performance. This lead to the design of simpler architectures instead of more complex architectures. The intention was to reach an optimization in the performance of a system rather than to optimize towards the minimization of the above-mentioned semantic gap. There were three major initial projects in this field: the 801 from IBM Research, the RISC I (and RISC II) from UCLA at Berkeley, and the MIPS from Stanford University. The technology, however, was grasped by the industry very quickly; a description of commercially available RISC processors can be found in [FURB 89], for example.

The basic idea of RISC architectures can probably be paraphrased by Einstein's word: *Make it as simple as possible, but not simpler*. This is reflected in a new set of architectural design principles, as they were described by Patterson [PATT 85]:

- Functions should be kept simple unless there is a very good reason to do otherwise.

- Microinstructions should not be faster than simple instructions.

- Microcode is not magic.

- Simple decoding and pipelined execution are more important than program size.

- Compiler technology should be used to simplify instructions rather than to generate complex instructions.

Thus, the concept of a reduced instruction set computer is not only to *reduce the total number* of instructions available (in general less than 100), but also to *simplify* the instructions with respect to same length and format and most of all only single cycle execution of all instructions. Besides, we find only a small number of addressing modes (e.g. two instead of 16 addressing modes for the VAX 11/780), a relatively large number of registers (e.g. 138 registers in the RISC II), and register-to-register operations (memory access is performed by load and store instructions only).

From a compiler's point of view RISC architectures mean:

- Reduction of complexity by selecting instructions for certain high level language constructs. RISC architectures often offer only one choice for selecting an instruction.

- More efficient code, because of a larger number of faster register-to-register operations instead of slow memory accesses. RISC architectures are based on the register-to-register execution model and, thus, forced the development of new techniques to minimize load and store operations.

- The usage of so-called *register windows* (see [PATT 85]) directly supports procedure calls and allows fast parameter passing. This and the above-mentioned new techniques reduce the proportion of data to instruction traffic considerable.

- Since RISC architectures are based on pipelined execution, a pipeline interlock management becomes necessary (if not done in hardware). In general, this is not a trivial task.

- Some RISC architectures confront compilers with delayed load, store, and branch instructions (e.g. IBM's 801). Thus, the compiler has to espy useful instructions which can be moved into the delay slot.

Some of these arguments show that RISC architectures cause new problems which cannot be overlooked by the compiler writer. Especially the generation of highly optimized code is not elementary; the code must be generated very accurately and carefully to avoid inefficiencies. In general, however, it can be stated that the compilation process for a RISC architecture is not more difficult than for a CISC architecture, since RISC architectures provide several features which make writing a compiler easier.

Exercises

(1) Design three regular grammars which generate

    (a)   PASCAL names;

    (b)   odd numbers;

    (c)   the language $L = \{ s^n \mid s \in \{01, 10\} \wedge n > 0 \}$.

Check the correctness of the production set.

(2) Let $A = \{a, b\}$ be the alphabet of the language L. Strings $w \in A^*$ that are accepted by L must fulfil the following conditions:

    i) $length(w) \geq 3$;

    ii)   the number of a's in w are twice as much than the number of b's.

E.g., aabaabaab $\in$ L, abab $\notin$ L.

Design

    (a)   a context-free grammar

    (b)   a context-sensitive grammar

which generate the language L. Check the correctness of the production set.

(3) Let the language L be defined as $L = \{ 0^n 1^{n-1} \mid n \geq 1 \}$. E.g., 0, 001, and 00011 are elements of L. Design a context-free grammar G (T, N, P, S) which generates L and where $|N| = 1$ and $|P| = 2$.

(4)   Given the ambiguous grammar G (T, N, P, S):

T: { 0, 1 }
N: { A, B }
P: { A   →   0BB
         B   →   1A | 0A | 0 }
S: A

Show the different syntax trees (parse trees) for a suitable word.

(5)   Given the grammar G (T, N, P, S) :

T   =   { 0, 1 }
N   =   { A, B, C }
P   =   { A   →   0 A B C | 0 1 C
             C B →   B C
             1 B →   1 1
             1 C →   1 }
S   =   { A }

(a)   What type of grammar is G (Chomsky-Hierarchy)? Proof.
(b)   Generate the smallest, the 2nd smallest, and the 3rd smallest word of
        the language L (G).
(c)   Give a set-definition of L(G).
(d)   Design a grammar G' (T, N', P', S) which generates L and where
        |N| = 1.

(6)   Given the grammar G (T, N, P, S) :

T   =   { id, +, (,) }
N   =   { E, T }
P   =   { E   →   T { + T }
             T   →   id | (E) }
S   =   { E }

Show the syntax graphs of G.

Note: Syntax graphs can be understood as analyzing algorithms. A sentence
is correct, when the elements of the sentence describe a complete path
through the graph.

(7)   Given the following part of the ALGOL60 grammar for statements describing
        the syntax of conditional statements:

stmt	→	uncond. stmt | cond. stmt | ...
cond. stmt	→	IFstmt [**ELSE** stmt]
uncond. stmt	→	basic stmt | compound stmt
IFstmt	→	**IF** log. expr. **THEN** uncond. stmt
basic stmt	→	assignment | goto stmt | proc stmt
compound stmt	→	**BEGIN** stmt **END**

(a)   Generate the syntax graphs for this grammar.

(b)   Generate a syntax tree for the following sentence:

IF *log. expr.* **THEN BEGIN IF** *log. expr.*
                                    THEN *assignment*
                                    ELSE *assginment*
                        END;

(c)   Why is the following sentence not correct?

IF *log. expr.* **THEN IF** *log. expr.*
                        THEN *assignment*
                        ELSE *assginment*

(8)   Design a regular grammar G which generates all sequences of 0 and 1,
        where the number of 0's and the number of 1's is even, and the length of the
        derivable strings is greater 1.

        Design a finite deterministic automaton which accepts L(G).

        Derive the sentence 010011011100 from the start symbol of the grammar
        and analyze that sentence with the automaton.

(9)   Design a finite automaton which recognizes real numbers of the form "123,
        123., 12.3, 12.E3, .123, .12E3, 12.3E3, 123E4." .

(10) Given the following finite automaton:

STATES	INPUT	
	0	1
I	A	B
A	E	B
B	A	E
E	E	E

where I is the initial state and { A, B } is the set of final states.

Generate the transition diagram of this automaton.

Which language will be accepted by the automaton?

Design a regular grammar for that language!

Analyze the following strings with the automaton:

           0101010
           0100101

(11) Design a finite deterministic automaton which accepts decimal numbers of the form "m.n or .n". Use the automaton to expand the lexical analysis of PL/0.

(12) Design a scanner for PL/0 in PASCAL which also accepts decimal numbers as defined in Exercise (11), which allows a PASCAL-like usage of comments, and which produces a compiler listing.

(13) Given the grammar G (T, N, P, S) :

T   =   { a, b, c, d }
N   =   { A, B, C }
P   =   { A   →   C B
           B   →   b C B | ε
           C   →   a | c A d }
S   =   { A }

Show that G is a LL(1)-grammar.

(14) Draw a diagram of a hash symbol table that would result when compiling the following example for the declaration of variable names:

```
REAL  x, y, z1, z2, z3;
INTEGER  i, j, k, last1;
STRING  Message;
BOOLEAN  ReadIS, Valve_Open;
ARRAY REAL  Valve (20);
ARRAY INTEGER  Max_Val (20);
```

Use the following hash function to code a word $w = w_1 w_2 ... w_k$:

$$H(w) \;=\; (ORD(w_1) + ORD(w_k) + 16^*k) \; MOD \; N + 1 \;,$$

assume a table size $N = 13$, and use *direct chaining* to generate secondary indices. (Note: Reserved words should not be included in this symbol table).

(15) Design a PASCAL-program handling hash symbol tables using the hash function of Exercise (14). Simulate a dynamic array, so that the address space can interactively be changed. Consider the names given in the variable names declaration example of Exercise (14) for different address spaces.
Make your program as simple as possible!

(16) Let G be a grammar, where none of the nonterminals can be derived to the empty string ε. Show that G is a LL(1)-grammar, if each alternative of a production starts with a different terminal.

(17) Design a LL(1)-grammar for the following language:

$$L(G) \;=\; \{ 0^n a 1^{2n} \mid n \geq 0 \}.$$

(18) Given a grammar G with the following productions:

$$
\begin{array}{rcl}
S & \rightarrow & AB \mid PQx \\
A & \rightarrow & xy \mid m \\
B & \rightarrow & bC \\
C & \rightarrow & bC \mid \varepsilon \\
P & \rightarrow & pP \mid \varepsilon \\
Q & \rightarrow & qQ \mid \varepsilon
\end{array}
$$

Is G a LL(1)-grammar? Give a reason for your answer.

(19) Explain why LL(1) grammars are not ambiguous.

(20) What properties of a grammar prevent the writing of a recursive descent parser from being straightforward?

(21) Write a recursive descent parser for *simple expressions* in Modula-2.

(22) Consider a grammar which is given by the following set of productions:

$$
\begin{array}{rcl}
S & \rightarrow & (A) \\
A & \rightarrow & CB \\
B & \rightarrow & ;A \mid \varepsilon \\
C & \rightarrow & x \mid S
\end{array}
$$

Construct the parse table for that grammar and analyze the sentence (x; (x)) using the parse table. Show the contents of the stack and the input buffer, as well as any production extracted from the parse table.

(23) Let $A = \{\, a_1, a_2, \dots , a_n \,\}$ be a set of n elements. Then, the set of lists $\in A^*$ can be defined as a formal language as follows:

- () is a list, i.e. the empty list;
- each $a \in A$ is a list;
- if $L_1, L_2, \dots , L_k$ are lists, then the concatenation $(L_1, L_2, \dots , L_k)$ is also a list.

Design an LL(1)-grammar which defines lists on A. Write a recursive descent parser for this grammar.

(24) Build an LL(1) parsing table for the language defined by the LL(1)-grammar having the productions (PROGRAM is the axiom)

PROGRAM → *begin d semi X end*
X   → *d semi X*
X   → *s Y*
Y   → ε
Y   → *semi s Y*

(25) Why is the grammar with the following productions not LL(1) (E is the axiom)? Convert this grammar into an LL(1)-grammar.

E → E + T
E → T
T → T*F
T → F
F → (E)
F → x
F → y

(26) Given the context-free grammar G (N, T, P, S) which generates logical expressions:

T = { **and, or, not,** (,), b }
N = { A, B, C }
P = { A → B | A **or** C
        B → C | B **and** C
        C → b | (A) | **not** C }
S = { A }

Why is G not a LL(1)-grammar?
Generate the parser tables for G (thereby proof that G is an SLR(1)-grammar).

(27) Consider the grammar

S → A S | b
A → S A | a

List all the LR(0)-items for the above grammar.

(28) Given the following grammar G (N, T, P, S):

$$
\begin{aligned}
T &= \{(,), a, \$\} \\
N &= \{A, B\} \\
P &= \{A &\rightarrow \$ B \$ \\
 & B &\rightarrow a \mid (B a)\} \\
S &= \{A\}
\end{aligned}
$$

Which language is generated by G?
Generate the parser tables for G.
Analyze the following sentences:

$$(())()$$
$$((())$$

(29) Given the following grammar G (N, T, P, S):

$$
\begin{aligned}
T &= \{a, f, z, [,], (,)\} \\
N &= \{E, I\} \\
P &= \{E &\rightarrow I(E) \mid I[E] \mid I \\
 & I &\rightarrow a \mid f \mid z\} \\
S &= \{E\}
\end{aligned}
$$

Generate the parser tables for G.
Analyze the following sentences:

$$f(a[z])$$
$$a[f[z]]$$

(30) The generation of the action table can lead to multiple entries indicating that the grammar is not SLR(1).
Show that the following grammar is not SLR(1):

$$
\begin{aligned}
S &\rightarrow E\$ \\
E &\rightarrow bEa \mid aEb \mid ba
\end{aligned}
$$

(31) Given the context-free grammar G (N, T, P, S) of Exercise (26). Define semantic actions for G's set of productions to generate

a)   postfix notation,
b)   three-address code.

Parse different sentences of L(G) and thereby generate the postfix notation and the three-address code for the selected sentences.

(32) Given the context-free grammar G (N, T, P, S) which generates logical expressions:

$$
\begin{aligned}
T &= \{a, b, c, d, e, f\} \\
N &= \{X, Y, Z\} \\
P &= \{X \rightarrow Y \mid X\,b\,Z \\
&\qquad\; Y \rightarrow Z \mid Y\,a\,Z \\
&\qquad\; Z \rightarrow f \mid d\,X\,e \mid c\,Z \} \\
S &= \{X\}
\end{aligned}
$$

Generate the parser tables for G (thereby proof that G is an SLR(1)-grammar). Analyze the sentence f a d f b c f e .

(33) Given the following arithmetic expressions:

$$
\begin{aligned}
&x + y - x\,{}^{*}y \\
&-x - y + x\,{}^{*}y \\
&u\,{}^{*}v\,{}^{*}w - x/y \\
&-(u\,{}^{*}v\,{}^{*}w - x/y) \\
&u\,{}^{*}(v\,{}^{*}w + x/w)
\end{aligned}
$$

Translate the expressions into postfix notation, three-address code, and two-address code.

(34) Design a compiler, which analyzes the syntax of arithmetic expressions and which generates postfix notation of these expressions.

(35) What is meant by strength and frequency reduction? Explain and give examples.

(36) Given the following code sequences. What are the corresponding arithmetic expressions?

a) Two-address code:

1	DIV	u	v
2	SUB	z	(1)
3	MUL	y	(2)
4	ADD	x	(3)
5	MUL	4	(4)
6	ADD	(5)	z

b) Postfix notation:

LOD 10
LOD A
MUL
LOD B
LOD C
MUL
ADD
LOD 3
LOD A
MUL
LOD B
DIV
SUB

(37) Indirect triples are often used to perform code optimization. In this case a separate table is used to indicate the order of execution for a sequence of triples. Optimization can then be performed by changing the order of the entries in the table. For example,

$$z := x + y - x * y$$
$$w := x * y$$

can be represented by indirect triples as follows:

Operations		Triples			
1. (1)		(1)	ADD	x	y
2. (2)		(2)	MUL	x	y
3. (3)		(3)	SUB	(1)	(2)
4. (4)		(4)	STO	(3)	z
5. (2)		(5)	STO	(2)	w
6. (5)					

Design an algorithm to detect and delete useless indirect triples.

(38) Expand the PL/0 grammar to allow an ELSE-part in conditional statements similar to the PASCAL-syntax. The semi-colon errors of Exercise (39) might also occur in this extension of PL/0. Legalize these errors by adding error production to the grammar.

(39) Given the following set of productions to generate "IF THEN" and "IF THEN ELSE" statements in MODULA-2:

stmt sequence	$\rightarrow$	*stmt*
stmt sequence	$\rightarrow$	*stmt sequence* ; *stmt*
stmt	$\rightarrow$	**IF** *log. expr.* **THEN** *stmt sequence* **END**
stmt	$\rightarrow$	**IF** *log. expr.* **THEN** *stmt sequence*
		ELSE *stmt sequence* **END**

A common syntax error in MODULA-2 is the usage of a semi-colon immediately followed by ELSE or END. Legalize those errors by expanding the above given set of productions by error productions.

(40) Given the following augmented grammar G(T, N, P, S) (the numbering of the productions will be used in the action-table):

$$
\begin{array}{lll}
T & = & \{ +, x, (,) \} \\
N & = & \{ E, T \} \\
P & = & \{ \ (0) \ \ S' \ \ \rightarrow \ \ E \\
& & \ \ \ \ (1) \ \ E \ \ \rightarrow \ \ T \\
& & \ \ \ \ (2) \ \ E \ \ \rightarrow \ \ E + T \\
& & \ \ \ \ (3) \ \ T \ \ \rightarrow \ \ (E) \\
& & \ \ \ \ (4) \ \ T \ \ \rightarrow \ \ x \ \} \\
S & = & \{ E \}
\end{array}
$$

The parse tables are given as follows:

	Action-table					Goto-table	
states	+	(	)	x	$	E	T
0		s3		s4		s1	s2
1	s5				accept		
2	p1		p1	p1	p1		
3		s3		s4		s6	s2
4	p4		p4	p4	p4		
5		s3		s4			s7
6	s5		s8				
7	p2		p2	p2	p2		
8	p3		p3	p3	p3		

Parse the sentence (x + x) + x using the LR-parse algorithm and the above given parse tables; describe for each step of the analysis the contents of stack and input buffer, as well as the executed actions.

References

[AHOS 86]   A. V. Aho, R. Sethi, J. D. Ullman. *Compilers - Principles, Techniques and Tools.* Addison-Wesley, Reading (1986).

[AHOU 73]   A. V. Aho, J. D. Ullman. *The Theory of Parsing, Translation, and Compiling. Volume I + II.* Prentice Hall, Englewood Cliffs (1973).

[ALLE 76]   F. E. Allen, J. Cocke. A program data flow analysis procedure. *CACM* 19 (1976), 137 - 147.

[BACK 78]   J. Backus. Can programming be liberated from the von Neumann style? A functional style and its algebra of programs. *CACM* 21 (1978), 613 - 641.

[BELA 66]   L. A. Belady. A study of replacement algorithms for a virtual storage computer. *IBM Systems Journal* 5 (1966).

[BELL 73]   J. R. Bell. Threaded Code. *CACM* 16 (1973), 370 - 372.

[BRIN 85]   P. Brinch Hansen. *Brinch Hansen on Pascal Compilers.* Prentice-Hall, Englewood Cliffs (1985).

[CICH 80]   R. J. Cichelli. Minimal perfect hash functions made simple. *CACM* 23 (1980), 17 - 19.

[FISC 88]   C. N. Fischer, R. J. LeBlanc. *Crafting a Compiler.* Benjamin/Cummings Publishing, Menlo Park (1988).

[FURB 89]   S. B. Furber. *VLSI RISC architecture and organization.* Marcel Dekker, New York (1989).

[JOHN 75]   S. C. Johnson. *Yacc - Yet Another Compiler-Compiler*. Comp. Sci. Tech. Report 32, AT&T Bell Labs, Murray Hill (1975).

[KUIC 86]   W. Kuich, A. Salomaa. *Semirings, Automata, Languages*. Springer-Verlag, Berlin (1986).

[LOEC 87]   J. Loeckx, K. Sieber. *The Foundations of Program Verification*. B. G. Teubner, Stuttgart, and John Wiley & Sons, New York (1987).

[MAUR 68]   W. D. Maurer. An Improved Hash Code for Scatter Storage. *CACM* **11** (1968), 35 - 38.

[MCKE 74]   W. M. McKeeman. Symbol Table Access. In: F. L. Bauer, J. Eickel (eds). Compiler Construction. *Lecture Notes in Computer Science*, Springer Verlag, Berlin (1974), 253 - 301.

[MCKE 89]   B. J. McKenzie. Fast Peephole Optimization Techniques. *Software - Practice and Experience* **19** (1989), 1151 - 1162.

[MILU 86]   V. Milutinovic (ed.). *Tutorial on Advanced Microprocessors and High-level Language Computer Architecture*. IEEE Computer Society Press, Los Alamitos (1986).

[MINS 67]   M. L. Minsky. *Computation: Finite and Infinite Machines*. Prentice-Hall, Englewood-Cliffs (1967).

[MORR 68]   R. Morris. Scatter Storage Techniques. *CACM* **11** (1968), 39 - 43.

[NAUR 63]   P. Naur (ed.). Revised Report on the Algorithmic Language ALGOL60. *CACM* **6** (1963), 1 - 17; *Comp. J.* **5** (1962/63), 349 - 367; *Num. Math.* **4** (1963), 420 - 453.

[NORI 81]   K. V. Nori, U. Amman, K. Jensen, H. H. Nägeli, Ch. Jacobi. Pascal-P Implementation Notes. In: D. W. Barron (ed.). *Pascal - The Language and Its Implementation*. John Wiley & Sons, New York (1981).

[PATT 85]   D. A. Patterson. Reduced instruction set computers. *CACM* **28** (1985), 8 - 21.

[RIPL 78]   D. G. Ripley, F. C. Druseikis. A Statistical Analysis of Syntax Errors. *Computer Languages* **3** (1978), 227 - 240.

[SALO 73]   A. K. Salomaa. *Formal Languages*. Academic Press, New York (1973).

[SUEN 79]   C. Y. Suen. n-Gram Statistics for Natural Language Understanding and Text Processing. *IEEE Trans. on Pattern Analysis and Machine Intelligence* **PAMI-1** (1979),164 - 172.

[TANE 82]   A. S. Tanenbaum, H. van Staveren, J. W. Stevenson. Using Peephole Optimization on Intermediate Code. *Trans. on Programming Languages and Systems* **4** (1982), 21 - 36.

[TEUF 84]   T. Teufel. A Hardware Architecture of an Optimal BCD-Floating-Point Processor. In: M. Feilmeier, J. Joubert, U. Schnedel (eds.): *Parallel Computing '83*, North-Holland, Amsterdam (1984).

[TEUF 86]   T. Teufel, G. Bohlender. A Bit-slice Processor Unit for Optimal Arithmetic. In: M. Ruschitzka (ed.): *Computer Systems: Performance and Simulation*, North-Holland, Amsterdam (1986).

[TEUF 91]   B. Teufel. *Organization of Programming Languages*. Springer-Verlag, New York (1991).

[TREM 85]   J. P. Tremblay, P. G. Sorenson. *The Theory and Practice of Compiler Writing*. McGraw-Hill, New York (1985).

[WAIT 84]   W. Waite, G. Goos. *Compiler Construction*. Springer-Verlag, New York (1984).

[WILK 51]   M. Wilkes. The Best Way to Design an Automatic Calculating Machine. *Proc. Manchester University Computer Inaugural Conference* (1951).

[WIRT 86]   N. Wirth. *Compilerbau*. B. G. Teubner Verlag, Stuttgart (1986).

[WIRT 76]   N. Wirth. *Algorithms + Data Structures = Programs*. Prentice-Hall, Englewood-Cliffs (1976).

[YAMA 81]   M. Yamamoto. A Survey of High-level Language Machines in Japan. *IEEE Computer* **14**(7) (1981), 68 - 77.

Index

Bernd Teufel

Organization of Programming Languages

1991. 50 figures. XI, 208 pages.
Soft cover DM 49,–, öS 345,–
ISBN 3-211-82315-8

Prices are subject to change without notice

The book is about high level programming languages, introducing the basic concepts that underlie various programming languages. Besides the evolution of programming languages, the most important aspects of language processing are considered. Elementary concepts from imperative programming languages are presented in terms of data types, expression and control structures, as well as procedures. Furthermore, the concepts of data encapsulation, inheritance, and concurrency are discussed in detail. The three major approaches to the description of semantics in programming languages are briefly introduced. The concepts of the programming languages are illustrated by examples from ADA, PASCAL, MODULA-2, OBERON, C++, SIMULA 67, SMALL-TALK-80, and EIFFEL. The examples are selected in a way which facilitates the comparison of the different approaches and features of those languages. The book was intended for a one session course on programming languages and, therefore, consists of many examples and exercises. It can be used both as a professional reference as well as a student text book.

Springer-Verlag Wien New York

A Min Tjoa, Isidro Ramos (eds.)

Database and Expert Systems Applications

Proceedings of the International Conference
in Valencia, Spain, 1992

1992. 324 figures. XIV, 541 pages.
Soft cover DM 148,-, öS 1036,-
ISBN 3-211-82400-6

Prices are subject to change without notice

The Database and Expert Systems Applications (DEXA) conferences are mainly oriented to establish a state-of-the-art forum on database and expert systems applications. But practice without theory has no sense, as Leonardo said five centuries ago. Therefore, as presented in this book, a compromise has been aimed at these two complementary aspects. Five sessions are application-oriented, ranging from classical applications to more unusual ones in software engineering. Actual research aspects in databases, such as activity, deductivity and/or object orientation are also presented in DEXA '92, as well as the implications of the new "data models" such as OO-model, deductive model, etc. are included in the modelling sessions.

Other areas of interest, such as hypertext and multimedia applications, together with the classical field of information retrieval are also considered. Finally, implementation aspects are reflected in very concrete fields.

Springer-Verlag Wien New York